how to meditate

how to meditate

A PRACTICAL GUIDE

second edition

Kathleen McDonald

Edited by Robina Courtin

Wisdom

Wisdom Publications
199 Elm Street
Somerville, Massachusetts 02144 USA
wisdomexperience.org

Library of Congress Cataloging-in-Publication Data
McDonald Kathleen, 1952–
 How to meditate : a practical guide / Kathleen McDonald ; edited by Robina Courtin. 2nd ed.
            p. cm.
    Includes bibliographical references and index.
    ISBN 0-86171-341-9
    1. Meditation. 2. Devotional exercises. I. Courtin, Robina. II. Title.
BQ5612 .M33 2006
294.3′443—22   2005033440

ISBN 978-0-86171-341-7   ebook ISBN 978-0-86171-984-6

24 23 22
11   10   9

Cover design by Philip Pascuzzo. Interior design by Roger Dormann. Set in Palatino 10/14 pt. All line drawings © Robert Beer. Painting on page 239 © Peter Iseli.

Contents

Preface

When *How to Meditate* was first published more than twenty years ago, meditation was not widely known or practiced in the West, and there were few books about it. Things are different now. Millions of Western people practice meditation regularly; doctors prescribe it to their patients as a way to deal with pain, heart disease, cancer, depression, and other problems; scientists are studying its effects on the brain and the immune system. There are dozens of books, tapes, CDs, and websites about meditation, and meditation classes are available in most cities.

This book has been surprisingly successful: reprinted seventeen times, translated into nine foreign languages. And I continue to meet people who tell me how it has helped them in their practice and their understanding of Buddhism and meditation. The purpose of this book remains the same as when it first appeared: to offer the people in the world today a bridge into the art of meditation taught by the Buddha and developed in Asia over the last 2500 years. Despite advances in technology, the Buddha's tools for opening up our inner capacities for genuine and lasting well-being retain their power and relevance.

Most of the meditations explained here come from the Mahayana Buddhist tradition of Tibet, several from the Theravada tradition of South East Asia, and a few are my own improvisations on Buddhist themes. I have tried to explain them simply and clearly, with a minimum of technical language, because I want to show that Buddhism is practical and down-to-earth, not a dry philosophy or an exotic cult. Throughout, the emphasis is on *experience,* using meditation to actually bring about changes in our thoughts, feelings, and actions.

Part 1, *Mind and Meditation,* lays the foundation, explaining why people meditate and how they benefit from it. Part 2, *Establishing a Meditation Practice,* gives basic information and advice for beginning practitioners. The rest of the book presents the actual meditation methods, divided into four parts: *Meditations on the Mind, Analytical Meditations, Visualization Meditations,* and *Prayers and Other Devotional Practices.* Each technique has a preamble that gives some background to the meditation, shows its benefits and how best to do it, and explains its practical application. Finally, there is a glossary of terms and a list of titles for suggested further reading.

For this present edition, I have revised most of the meditations and added several new ones: on karma, purifiying negative karma, compassion and *tonglen* (Tibetan for "giving and taking"), and the Healing Buddha. The revisions do not mean that the meditations in the original edition are incorrect; I simply felt that they could be improved, based on an additional twenty years of practicing and teaching meditation.

Acknowledgments

Whatever I know about Buddhism and meditation I have learned from my kind and compassionate teachers, especially Lama Thubten Yeshe, Zopa Rinpoche, His Holiness the Dalai Lama, Geshe Ngawang Dhargyey, Geshe Jampa Tegchog, and Ribur Rinpoche.

I thank these precious teachers from my heart for sharing with us their knowledge and insight and pray sincerely that their work may continue for a long time to come.

Many people have worked to make this book possible. I extend thanks to Wendy Finster for her *Handbook of Mahayana Practices,* from which this book developed; to Thubten Wongmo, Jon Landaw, and T. Yeshe for their initial editing and translating work; to Nick Ribush, Yeshe Khadro, Thubten Pende, Steve Carlier, Lorraine Rees, Peter Rees, James Payne, Tim Young, Jan Courtin,

Marshall Harris, Sarah Thresher, Karin Zeitvogel, and the nuns of Dorje Pamo Monastery for their invaluable suggestions; to David Kittelstrom, Tim McNeill, and everyone at Wisdom Publications; and finally to my editor Robina Courtin, who has worked with me throughout both editions to rewrite and reshape *How to Meditate* in an effort to make it as clear and practical as possible.

For my parents who have helped me so much.
May they discover the highest peace within themselves.

Part One

MIND AND MEDITATION

1

Why Meditate?

Everyone wants happiness yet few of us seem to find it. In our search for satisfaction we go from one relationship to another, one job to another, one country to another. We study art and medicine, train to be tennis players and typists; have babies, race cars, write books, and grow flowers. We spend our money on home entertainment systems, mobile phones, iPods, handheld computers, comfortable furniture, and vacations in the sun. Or we try to get back to nature, eat whole foods, practice yoga, and meditate. Just about everything we do is an attempt to find real happiness and avoid suffering.

There is nothing wrong with wanting happiness; there is nothing wrong with any of these attempts to find it. The problem is that we see things like relationships, possessions, and adventures as having some intrinsic ability to satisfy us, as being the cause of happiness. But they cannot be—simply because they do not last. Everything by nature constantly changes and eventually disappears: our body, our friends, all our belongings, the environment. Our dependence on impermanent things and our clinging to the rainbow-like happiness they bring cause only disappointment and grief, not satisfaction and contentment.

We *do* experience happiness with things outside ourselves, but it doesn't truly satisfy us or free us from our problems. It is poor-quality happiness, unreliable and short-lived. This does not mean that we should give up our friends and possessions in order to be happy. Rather, what we need to give up are our misconceptions about them and our unrealistic expectations of what they can do for us.

Not only do we see them as permanent and able to satisfy us; at the root of our problems is our fundamentally mistaken view of reality. We believe instinctively that people and things exist in and of themselves, from their own side; that they have an inherent nature, an inherent thing-ness. This means that we see things as having certain qualities abiding naturally within them; we think that they are, from their own side, good or bad, attractive or unattractive. These qualities seem to be out there, in the objects themselves, quite independent of our viewpoint and everything else. We think, for example, that chocolate is inherently delicious or that success is inherently satisfying. But surely, if they were, they would never fail to give pleasure or to satisfy, and everyone would experience them in the same way.

Our mistaken idea is deeply ingrained and habitual; it colors all our relationships and dealings with the world. We probably rarely question whether the way we see things is the way they actually exist, but once we do it will be obvious that our picture of reality is exaggerated and one-sided; that the good and bad qualities we see in things are actually created and projected by our own mind.

According to Buddhism there *is* lasting, stable happiness, and everyone has the potential to experience it. The causes of happiness lie within our own mind, and methods for achieving it can be practiced by anyone, anywhere, in any lifestyle—living in the city, working an eight-hour job, raising a family, playing on weekends.

By practicing these methods—meditation—we can learn to be happy at any time, in any situation, even difficult and painful ones. Eventually we can free ourselves of problems like dissatisfaction, anger, and anxiety and, finally, by realizing the actual way that things exist, we will eliminate completely the very source of all disturbing states of mind so that they will never arise again.

What is the mind?

Mind, or consciousness, is at the heart of Buddhist theory and practice, and for the last 2500 years meditators have been investigating and using it as a means of transcending unsatisfactory existence and achieving perfect peace. It is said that all happiness, ordinary and sublime, is achieved by understanding and transforming our own minds.

The mind is a nonphysical kind of energy, and its function is to know, to experience. It is awareness itself. It is clear in nature and reflects everything that it experiences, just as a still lake reflects the surrounding mountains and forests.

Mind changes from moment to moment. It is a beginningless continuum, like an ever-flowing stream: the previous mind-moment gave rise to this mind-moment, which gives rise to the next mind-moment, and so on. It is the general name given to the totality of our conscious and unconscious experiences: each of us is the center of a world of thoughts, perceptions, feelings, memories, and dreams—all of these are mind.

Mind is not a physical thing that *has* thoughts and feelings; it *is* those very experiences. Being nonphysical, it is different from the body, although mind and body are interconnected and interdependent. Mind—consciousness—is carried through our body by subtle physical energies (see page 161), which also control our movement and vital functions. This relationship explains why, for example, physical sickness and discomfort can affect our state of mind and why, in turn, mental attitudes can both give rise to and heal physical problems.

Mind can be compared to an ocean, and momentary mental events such as happiness, irritation, fantasies, and boredom to the waves that rise and fall on its surface. Just as the waves can subside to reveal the stillness of the ocean's depths, so too is it possible to calm the turbulence of our mind to reveal its natural pristine clarity.

The ability to do this lies within the mind itself, and the key to the mind is meditation.

2
What Is Meditation?

Subduing the mind and bringing it to the right understanding of reality is no easy task. It requires a slow and gradual process of *listening* to and reading explanations of the mind and the nature of things; *thinking* about and carefully analyzing this information; and finally transforming the mind through *meditation*.

The mind can be divided into *sense consciousness*—sight, hearing, smell, taste, and touch—and *mental consciousness*. Mental consciousness ranges from our grossest experiences of anger or desire, for example, to the subtlest level of complete stillness and clarity. It includes our intellectual processes, our feelings and emotions, our memory, and our dreams.

Meditation is an activity of the mental consciousness. It involves one part of the mind observing, analyzing, and dealing with the rest of the mind. Meditation can take many forms: concentrating single-pointedly on an (internal) object, trying to understand some personal problem, generating a joyful love for all humanity, praying to an object of devotion, or communicating with our own inner wisdom. Its ultimate aim is to awaken a very subtle level of consciousness and to use it to discover reality, directly and intuitively.

This direct, intuitive awareness of how things are, combined with love and compassion for all beings, is known as enlightenment and is the end result of Mahayana Buddhist practice. The purpose of reaching it—and the driving force behind all practice—is to help others reach it too.

The Tibetan term for meditation, *gom*, means, literally, "to become familiar." What arises in our mind is what we are most familiar with. If, when someone treats us unkindly or disrespect-fully, we immediately feel hurt or angry, it is because these are the reactions that we are most familiar with, or habituated to. Buddhist meditation involves making our mind familiar with positive states such as love, compassion, patience, serenity, and wisdom, so that these become more natural and spontaneous. Then, when we encounter an unkind or hostile person, we'll be more likely to remain calm and patient, and even feel compassion for them.

There are many different techniques of meditation; each technique has specific functions and benefits, and each is a part of the frame-work for bringing our mind to a more realistic view of the world.

It might be best to start by saying what meditation is *not*, because there are many misunderstandings about it. For one thing, med-itation is not an activity of the body: it is not simply a matter of sitting in a particular posture or breathing a particular way, nor is it done for the purpose of experiencing pleasant bodily sensations. Rather, it is an activity of the mind, and is done for the purpose of transforming the mind, making it more positive. Although the best results usually come when we meditate sitting in a quiet place, we can also meditate in a noisy environment, and while working, walking, riding on a bus, or cooking dinner. One Tibetan meditator realized emptiness while chopping wood, and another attained single-pointed concentration while cleaning his teacher's room.

First, we learn to develop the meditative state of mind in formal, sitting practice, but once we are good at it, we can be more freestyle and creative and can generate this mental state at any time, in any situation. By then, meditation has become a way of life.

Meditation is not something foreign or unsuitable for the Western mind. There are different methods practiced in different cultures, but they all share the common principle of the mind simply becom-ing familiar with positive, beneficial states. And the mind of every person, Eastern or Western, has the same basic elements and expe-riences, the same basic problems—and the same potential.

Meditation is not spacing-out or running away. In fact, it is being totally honest with ourselves: taking a good look at what we are and working with that in order to become more positive

and useful, to ourselves and others. There are both positive and
negative aspects of the mind. The negative aspects—our mental
disorders or, quite literally, delusions—include jealousy, anger,
desire, pride, and the like. These arise from our misunderstanding
of reality and habitual clinging to the way we see things. Through
meditation we can recognize our mistakes and adjust our mind to
think and react more realistically, more honestly.

The final goal, enlightenment, is a long-term one. But meditations
done with this goal in mind can and do have enormous short-term
benefits. As our concrete picture of reality softens, we develop a
more positive and realistic self-image and are thus more relaxed
and less anxious. We learn to have fewer unrealistic expectations
of the people and things around us and therefore meet with less
disappointment; relationships improve and life becomes more
stable and satisfying.

But remember, lifelong habits die hard. It is difficult enough
simply to recognize our anger and jealousy, much less make an
effort to hold back the old familiar tide of feeling or analyze its
causes and results. Transforming the mind is a slow and gradual
process. It is a matter of ridding ourselves, bit by bit, of instinctive,
harmful habit patterns and "becoming familiar" with habits that
necessarily bring positive results—to ourselves and others.

There are many meditation techniques but, according to the
Tibetan tradition, all can be classsed into two categories: *stabilizing*
and *analytical.*

Stabilizing meditation

In general, this type of meditation is used to develop concentration,
and eventually to attain calm abiding (Sanskrit: *shamata*), a special
kind of concentration that enables one to remain focused on whatever object one wishes, for as long as one wishes, while experiencing bliss, clarity, and peace. Concentration and calm abiding are
necessary for any real, lasting insight and mental transformation.
In stabilizing meditation, we learn to concentrate upon one object—

the breath, the nature of one's own mind, a concept, a visualized image—without interruption.

Concentration without interruption is the exact opposite of our usual state of mind. If you turn inward for a few moments you will notice your mind jumping from one thing to another: a thought of something you will do later, a sound outside, a friend, something that happened earlier, a physical sensation, a cup of coffee. We never need to say to the mind, "Think!" or "Feel!" It is always busy doing something, speeding along, with an energy of its own.

With such a scattered and uncontrolled mind there is little chance of success in anything we do, whether it is remembering a telephone number, cooking a meal, or running a business. And certainly, without concentration successful meditation is impossible.

Stabilizing meditation is not easy, but it is essential for bringing the mind under control. Although the development of actual single-pointed concentration and calm abiding is the work of full-time meditators, we don't need to retreat to the mountains to experience the benefits of this kind of meditation: even in our day-to-day city life we can develop good concentration by regularly doing ten or fifteen minutes a day of stabilizing meditation (for example, the meditation on the breath, page 37). It can bring an immediate sense of spaciousness and allow us to see the workings of our mind more clearly, both during the meditation and throughout the rest of the day.

Analytical meditation

This type of meditation is for the purpose of developing insight, or correct understanding of the way things are, and eventually to attain special insight (Sanskrit: *vipashyana*) that sees the ultimate nature of all things. Analytical meditation brings into play creative, intellectual thought and is crucial to our development: the first step in gaining any real insight is to understand *conceptually* how things are. This conceptual clarity develops into firm conviction which, when combined with stabilizing meditation, brings direct and intuitive knowing.

However, even before we can "know how things are" we must first identify our wrong conceptions. Using clear, penetrative, analytical thought we unravel the complexities of our attitudes and behavior patterns. Gradually, we can eliminate those thoughts, feelings, and ideas that cause ourselves and others unhappiness, and in their place cultivate thoughts, feelings, and ideas that bring happiness and peace.

In this way we become familiar with the reality of, for example, cause and effect—that our present experiences are the result of our past actions *and* the cause of our future experiences—or with the fact that all things lack an inherent nature. We can meditate point by point on the benefits of patience and the disadvantages of anger; on the value of developing compassion; on the kindness of others.

In one sense, an analytical meditation session is an intensive study session. However, the level of conceptual thought that we can reach during these meditations is more subtle and therefore more potent than our thoughts during day-to-day life. Because our senses are not being bombarded by the usual frantic input we are able to concentrate more strongly and develop a finely-tuned sensitivity to the workings of our mind.

Analytical meditation can also be used as self-therapy. Lama Yeshe said, "Each of us should know our own mind; you should become your own psychologist." When we have a problem or we feel emotionally upset, we can sit down and make our mind calmer with a few minutes of meditation on the breath. Then, taking a step back from our thoughts and emotions, we can try to understand what's going on. "What kind of thoughts are going through my mind? What emotions are arising?" Within the calm, clear space of meditation, it will be easier to recognize where our thinking is erroneous and to adjust it by bringing in more realistic and beneficial ideas that we have learned from our spiritual study and practice.

Some people think that meditation is necessarily stabilizing, or single-pointed, meditation, and that when we meditate, our mind should be free of all thoughts and concepts. This is not correct: single-pointed meditation is *not* the only kind of meditation there is, and thoughts and concepts, when used skillfully, play a crucial role in the positive transformation of our mind. At the root of our problems and confusion are mistaken concepts about reality, and the only way to be free from these is to first identify and transform them by using analytical meditation. Staying focused on these new insights with single-pointedness enables the mind to become thoroughly and deeply familiar with them. This is how real, lasting transformation of the mind takes place.

Stabilizing and analytical meditations, then, are complementary and can be used together in one session. When doing a meditation on emptiness, for example, we analyze the object (emptiness) using information we have heard or read, as well as our own thoughts, feelings, and memories. At some point an intuitive experience of or conviction about the object arises. We should then stop thinking and focus our attention single-pointedly on the feeling for as long as possible. We should soak our mind in the experience. When the feeling fades we can either continue analyzing or conclude the session.

This method of combining the two kinds of meditation causes the mind literally to become one with the object of meditation. The stronger our concentration, the deeper our insight will be. We need to repeat this process again and again with anything we want to understand in order to transform our insight into actual experience.

Stabilizing meditations such as the meditation on the breath will also go better if some skillful analysis is used. When we sit down to meditate, we should start by examining our state of mind and clarifying our motivation for doing the practice, and this involves analytical thought. During the meditation itself we might find concentration especially difficult; at such times it is good to analyze the problem for a few moments, then to re-place the mind on the breath. And sometimes it is useful to check on the mind during the meditation to make sure it is not daydreaming but doing what it is supposed to be doing.

The meditations in this book are divided into four sections. The first of these, *Meditations on the Mind*, includes three techniques that help develop awareness of the mind itself. The meditation on the breath (often called *mindfulness meditation*) is primarily a stabilizing practice that uses the breath as the object of concentration. Beginners are advised to start with this practice, as it calms the mind, enabling us to see more clearly how it works.

The other meditations in this section are for developing an awareness of the clear nature of the mind, and the beginning-lessness and continuity of the mind. All techniques involve both stabilization and analysis.

The next section, *Analytical Meditations,* offers eleven techniques for looking into and analyzing our assumptions about how things exist, about life, death, suffering, and compassion; and, finally, advice on dealing with our negative energy in everyday life. If you are just learning to slow the mind down with, say, the breathing meditation, you might not feel ready to tackle any of these sub-jects in formal meditation; however, simply reading through this section provides plenty of food for thought.

Next is *Visualization Meditations:* five techniques introduce visualization as used in tantric Vajrayana practice; all combine stabilization and analysis.

The final section of the main body of the book, *Prayers and Other Devotional Practices*, includes several more meditations as well as prayers and other practices.

It is important to go slowly and to adopt new methods only when you are ready. There is no point in trying to do meditations that seem strange or complicated or whose purpose is not clear. It is better to stick to one or two methods whose benefits you can really experience.

However, everything in this book is an integral part of balanced spiritual growth and a step on a path that is vast and profound. For example, most of the analytical meditations are from the graduated path (Tibetan: *lamrim*) tradition, a well-organized series of topics to be learned, contemplated, and integrated experientially, a process that gets us from our present unenlightened state to the fulfillment of our potential for perfection: enlightenment. (For more informa-tion about the graduated path, see the recommended reading list at the end of the book.)

Through careful and patient study and practice, you will learn to appreciate the relationship that these practices have to each other and to the entire path.

Part Two

ESTABLISHING A
MEDITATION
PRACTICE

1
Advice for Beginners

Regular practice

In order to experience the benefits of meditation it is necessary to practice regularly; as with any activity, it is not possible to succeed unless we dedicate our energy wholeheartedly to it. Try to meditate every day, or at least several times a week. If you let weeks or months pass without meditating you will get out of shape and find it all the more difficult when you try again. Inevitably there will be times when the last thing you want to do is meditate, but meditate anyway, even for only a few minutes; often these sessions are the most productive.

The meditation place

If possible, it is best to reserve a room or corner especially for your meditation sessions.

Set up your seat, either a cushion on the floor, on a bed or sofa, or a straight-backed chair, with a table or low bench in front of you for this and other books that you need for your meditations.

If you are so inclined you can set up an altar nearby for statues or pictures that inspire you, and for offerings to the Buddhas such as candles, incense, flowers, and fruit.

Ideally, the place should be clean and quiet, where you won't be disturbed. However, with discipline it is possible to meditate in a crowded, noisy environment; people in prison, for example, often cannot find a quiet place and still become successful meditators. Even if your surroundings are busy and noisy, make your meditation place as pleasing and comfortable as possible, so that you are happy to be there and can't wait to return!

Choosing a practice

It is good to start with the meditation on the breath (page 37). This is ideal for calming the mind and starting to develop some insight into your thoughts and feelings—and both calm and insight are essential ingredients for successful meditations of any kind.

Once you're familiar with meditation, choose the practices that best suit your needs, remembering that all the techniques here are either antidotes to particular problems or methods for enhancing particular qualities. If, for example, you are inclined toward anger, you could meditate on patience (page 129) or loving-kindness (page 111). If disturbed by strong desire or attachment, you would benefit from meditating on impermanence (page 65), death (page 69), or suffering (page 97). Depression can be counteracted by thinking about the preciousness and potential of your human life (page 59). Often we feel that things happen randomly or that life is unfair: if so, meditate on karma (page 80). If you regret the harm you have done to others or feel hopeless and don't believe you can change, do one of the purification practices (pages 90, 148, or 219). If you're overwhelmed by the suffering of the world and want to develop the courage to help others, meditate on compassion and tonglen (page 116).

When your mind is tranquil, it's good to develop concentration with a visualization technique that appeals to you (page 143), or deepen your insight into the meaning of reality by meditating on emptiness (page 53). If you appreciate the benefits of devotional practices, you can incorporate prostrations and prayers (page 167) or choose a visualization meditation.

All this is meant as a general guide only; with practice you will learn to know what to do when. However, the importance of being guided by an experienced meditator cannot be over-emphasized (see page 18).

Short sessions

In the beginning it is best to meditate for short periods—ten to thirty minutes—and end your session while mind and body are still comfortable and fresh. If you push yourself to meditate for too long and rise from your seat with an aching body and a frustrated mind, you won't have much interest in sitting down to meditate again. Meditation should be a satisfying and productive experience, not a burden.

You should decide beforehand on a period of time for the session and stick to it, even if the meditation is going well. As your skill develops you can increase the length of your sessions accordingly.

Be relaxed but alert

Mind and body should be relaxed and comfortable throughout the session. You can relax mentally by firmly deciding to leave behind all problems, worries and involvements of the external world and immerse yourself in your inner world. It might help to recall a past experience of feeling at ease and contented—and then generate that same feeling on your meditation seat.

Breathing meditation can also bring the same result. Observing the gentle, natural rhythm of the breath and avoiding distracting thoughts, your mental state gradually becomes tranquil and clear. But don't fall asleep! Stay alert. Take note of whatever thoughts, images, feelings, and sensations arise in your mind without becoming involved in them. Your main focus of attention should always be the breath (or whatever subject you have chosen to meditate on).

Physical relaxation can be facilitated by the practice of such disciplines as yoga, tai chi, kum nye, or other stress reduction and relaxation methods. Any means you use to ease physical tension and improve your ability to sit in meditation is a valuable addition to your practice.

No expectations

Since we all want to enjoy happiness and peace of mind and avoid problems, it is natural to want good experiences during meditation. But such expectations are not necessarily realistic and are likely to hinder your progress. The mind is complex and ever-changing. One day you might have a calm, joyful meditation and the next a meditation beset by distractions and turmoil. This is quite normal and should not cause worry or frustration. Be ready for anything and do not be disturbed by whatever happens. The most troublesome painful experiences can be the most valuable in terms of the growth of wisdom.

Feel satisfied that you are making the effort to meditate and transform your mind—that itself is meditation. As long as you are trying, it is mistaken to think that you can't meditate. Results take time. Don't be discouraged if you have not achieved good concentration within a few weeks; it is better to think in terms of years. Habits built up over a lifetime are not eliminated instantly but by gradual cultivation of new habits. So be easy on yourself. Recognize your capabilities and limitations and evaluate your progress accordingly.

The need for a teacher

The most effective way to learn anything is to study with someone who has already mastered it—and meditation is no exception. The mind can be compared to a musical instrument: in order to create beautiful music with it we need to study with a master who knows the instrument inside and out, and in order to develop a clear, enthusiastic, and loving mind we need the guidance of someone who thoroughly understands how the mind works and how it can be transformed.

However, it is not easy to find a qualified teacher. The qualities to look for include compassion, knowledge and insight, morality, sincerity, and skill in explanation. You should have confidence in your teacher and communicate well with him or her. Therefore, it might be a matter of years before you meet the right teacher. But don't think you should set out on a frantic guru hunt! Take it easy. When the time is right you will meet the person who can guide you successfully.

In the meantime, you can practice meditations such as those explained here, and seek the advice of any practitioner whose qualities you admire—even if the person has been meditating for only a short time. Your own innate wisdom, your inner guru, will tell you whether or not you are heading in the right direction.

Don't advertise!

Whenever we discover something new and interesting we feel like telling everyone about it, but it is not a good idea to talk too much about your meditation. Unless someone is sincerely interested and asks you about it, it is better to keep quiet. Broadcasting your experiences will dissipate whatever good energy and insight you have gained. It is best to discuss your practice only with your teacher and a few close friends.

Having taken up meditation there is no need to make big changes in your lifestyle, behavior, or appearance. You can keep your job and your friends, continue to live in your nice house, and just enjoy life as usual.

Meditation is an internal, not external, activity. Your practice will transform your mind on a subtle level, making you more sensitive and clear, and giving you fresh insight into ordinary day-to-day experiences. Superficial changes are not natural and are unlikely to impress anyone, but the deep, natural changes created by meditation are real and beneficial, both for yourself and others.

2

The Meditation Session

Sit

Sit comfortably in either the seven-point posture or some other recommended position (see page 24). Spend a few minutes settling your body and mind. Decide which meditation you will do and for how long you will meditate, and determine not to do anything else for that period of time.

It is traditional to prostrate three times before sitting down to meditate (see page 177). Prostration counteracts pride. It expresses our acceptance that we have work to do, problems to solve, and a long way to go in our inner development. It is not necessarily an act of submission to something external, but a recognition that the potential for wholeness and perfection lies within us. We are prostrating to our own true nature, which we want to awaken through meditation. If done with this understanding, prostration helps put the mind in the right state for meditation.

Motivate

Check up on your thoughts. Why do you want to meditate? What do you hope to achieve? As with any activity, the clearer and more firmly we set our goal, the stronger is our motivation and the more likely we are to succeed.

A short-term goal of meditation is simply to calm down and relax. More far-reaching is the aim eventually to penetrate through to a complete understanding of the nature of reality as an antidote to unhappiness and dissatisfaction. However, the most altruistic and thus the highest aim of meditation is to achieve enlightenment in order to help others gain it, too. This aspiration is known in Sanskrit as *bodhichitta*. It is the most far-reaching objective—the Mahayana motivation—and inevitably the other goals will be reached on the way. If you are comfortable with this idea, you can start your meditation by thinking: "I am going to do this meditation in order to attain enlightenment so that I can help all beings attain that state as well."

However, it may be difficult for you to think that your reason for meditating is to attain enlightenment—this goal may seem too vast or far-distant for you to realistically consider—but you may still have an altruistic wish to be more beneficial to others. In that case you could think something like this: "I wish to practice meditation in order to decrease the negative energy in my mind— anger, self-centeredness, attachment, pride, and so forth—and to increase my positive qualities such as love, compassion, patience, and wisdom. In this way, I will have more beneficial, positive energy to bring into my interactions with others, and to send out into the world."

Whichever your motivation, think it through clearly before proceeding with your meditation.

If you feel it would help your practice you can say either all the preliminary prayers on pages 171–74 or just the prayer of refuge and bodhichitta. Some people find that reciting prayers, either mentally or verbally, induces a good frame of mind for meditation by reminding them of the wisdom and other qualities they want to achieve. If you do pray, reflect on the meaning of each prayer so that it flows naturally from your heart.

Meditate

Now, turn to the object of meditation and keep it firmly in mind throughout the period. Follow the advice in the chapter starting on page 27 if you come up against problems during the session.

If you do a stabilizing meditation—for example, focusing on the breath—aim to hold your mind unwaveringly on the object of concentration.

If you do an analytical meditation, investigate the topic with full attention until an intuitive feeling of it arises, then place your mind single-pointedly—in other words, do stabilizing meditation—on that insight so that it becomes literally one with your experience. When the feeling or your concentration starts to fade, return to the analytical process.

Before starting the meditation it is important to read the preamble and then to integrate into the meditation—especially analytical meditation—the ideas raised there.

End the meditation with a firm conclusion about the topic, based on your insight and experiences during the session.

Ideally, of course, it would be best not to need to refer to this or other books during your meditation, but until you know the details you cannot avoid having to open your eyes from time to time to check on the next stage of the meditation. Experiment to find the most comfortable way to conduct your sessions.

It is very useful to follow the meditations on a CD or MP3 player, or to take it in turns with a fellow meditator to read out the meditations to each other.

Whichever method you use, the important point is to be relaxed and free of all unrealistic expectations about the way you think the session should go. Follow the instructions—and your own wisdom—as well as you can, don't panic, and have confidence!

Dedicate

Every time you meditate, even for just a few minutes, you create positive energy and develop some degree of insight. The effects of this energy and insight are determined by your thoughts and attitudes as you move from meditation to ordinary activity. If you finish the session in an unhappy frame of mind or rush off too quickly, much of the energy is likely to be lost.

Before you leave your meditation seat, take a few minutes to recall your reasons and motivation for doing the session and dedicate your energy and insight to the fulfillment of these objectives.

Clear dedication in this way stabilizes the insight and ensures that results come. (See page 174 for dedication prayers.)

And don't forget to bring the good experiences of the meditation into your daily activities. Instead of acting and reacting impulsively and following your thoughts and feelings here and there, watch your mind carefully, be aware, and try to deal skillfully with problems as they arise. If you can do this every day, your meditation has been successful.

3
Posture

Mind and body are interdependent. Because the state of one affects the state of the other, a correct sitting posture is emphasized for meditation. The seven-point posture, used by experienced meditators for centuries, is recommended as the best.

Legs

The best position for meditation is the vajra, or full-lotus, position, where you sit cross-legged with each foot placed, sole upward, on the thigh of the opposite leg. This position is difficult for many people, but practicing yoga or stretching exercises may loosen your legs enough to be able to sit this way for a short time, and continued practice will enable you to maintain it for increasingly longer periods. The vajra posture gives the best support to the body, but is not essential, so don't worry if you are unable to do it.

An alternative position is the half-lotus where the left foot is on the floor under the right leg and the right foot on top of the left thigh. You can also sit in a simple cross-legged posture with both feet on the floor.

Having a mat or carpet beneath you and a cushion or two under your buttocks will enable you to sit comfortably for longer periods, with a straight back, and avoid numbness in your legs and feet.

If you are unable to sit in any of these cross-legged positions, you can meditate in a chair or on a low, slanted bench. The important thing is to be comfortable.

Arms

Hold your hands loosely on your lap, about two inches below the navel, right hand on top of the left, palms upward, with the fingers aligned. The two hands should be slightly cupped so that the tips of the thumbs meet to form a triangle. Shoulders and arms should be relaxed. Your arms should not be pressed against your body but held a few inches away to allow circulation of air: this helps to prevent sleepiness.

Back

Your back is most important. It should be straight, held relaxed and lightly upright, as if the vertebrae were a pile of coins. It might be difficult in the beginning, but in time it will become natural and you will notice the benefits: your energy will flow more freely (see page 161), you won't feel sluggish, and you will be able to sit comfortably in meditation for increasingly longer periods.

Eyes

New meditators often find it easier to concentrate with their eyes fully closed. This is quite acceptable. However, it is recommended that you leave your eyes slightly open to admit a little light, and direct your gaze downward. Closing your eyes may be an invitation to sluggishness, sleep, or dream-like images, all of which hinder meditation.

Jaw

Your jaw should be relaxed and teeth slightly apart, not clenched. Your mouth should also be relaxed, with the lips together lightly.

Tongue

The tip of your tongue should touch the palate just behind the upper teeth. This reduces the flow of saliva and thus the need to swallow, both of which could be distracting as your concentration increases and you sit in meditation for longer periods.

Head

Your neck should be bent forward a little so that your gaze is directed naturally toward the floor in front of you. If your head is held too high you may have problems with mental wandering and agitation, and if dropped too low you could experience mental heaviness or sleepiness.

This seven-point posture is most conducive to clear, unobstructed contemplation. You might find it difficult in the beginning, but it is a good idea to check every point at the start of your session and try to maintain the correct posture for a few minutes. With familiarity it will feel more natural and you will begin to notice its benefits.

The practice of hatha yoga or other physical disciplines can be a great help in loosening tight muscles and joints, thus enabling you to sit more comfortably. However, if you are unable to adapt to sitting cross-legged you can make a compromise between perfect posture and a relaxed state. In other words, keep your body and mind happy, comfortable, and free of tension.

4

Common Problems

Restlessness and distractions

At times during a meditation session the mind is very restless and our attention is continually distracted by other things. These can include external objects like sounds, but also internal distractions such as memories of the past, fantasies about the future, or incessant chatter about what's happening in the present. Such thoughts are often accompanied by disturbing emotions, such as attachment (grasping at pleasant experiences); anger or hatred (obsessing over what someone did that hurt or irritated us); fear; doubt; jealousy; or depression. Normally we just let the mind run like this without trying to control it, so mental wandering has become a deeply ingrained habit.

It is not easy to give up habits, but we should recognize that this one—this mental excitement, as it's called—is the very opposite of meditation. As long as we are busy running in circles on the surface of the mind we will never penetrate to its depths and never develop the concentration we need for perceiving reality.

There are a number of methods for counteracting mental excitement. One is to focus firmly on the breath and let the mind become as calm and even as the natural rhythm of your breathing (see page 37). Every time your attention wanders, bring it back to the breath. Observe whatever thoughts and feelings arise without getting involved in them; recall that they are just waves of your mind, rising and falling. But if your mind is strongly caught up in a disturbing emotion such as attachment or anger, it might be necessary to spend some time working with one or more of the antidotes to these (see page 122). Once you have regained control over your mind you can return to the main object of the session.

An effective method from the Tibetan tradition for calming the mind is known as the Nine-Round Breathing Practice. This can be used at the beginning of a meditation session, or in the middle of a session, if your mind gets out of control.

1. For the first three breaths, breathe in through the right nostril and out through the left. If you wish, you can use your forefinger to close the left nostril while you breathe in and to close the right when you breathe out.
2. For the next three breaths, breathe in through the left nostril and out through the right. Again, you can use your forefinger to close the nostril you are not using.
3. For the last three breaths, breathe in through both nostrils and out through both.

With each breath, keep your mind focused on the breath and on the sensations you can feel at the nostrils as the breath goes in and out. Do not let your mind be distracted by thoughts or anything else. You can repeat the nine rounds several times if you wish, then return to your main meditation practice.

Another method recommended by Tibetan yogis is to imagine that the mind is enclosed within a tiny round seed whose upper hemisphere is white and whose lower hemisphere is red, situated in the central channel (see page 161) at the level of your navel. Concentrate on this until the mind has quieted down, then return to the object of meditation.

If you are familiar with the analytical meditations on death, impermanence, or suffering (see part 4), think briefly over the essential points of any one of these; this often helps to make your mind more calm and balanced. It might also help to recall your motivation—why you sat down to meditate in the first place—and thus strengthen your determination.

If mental restlessness is a recurring problem, check your posture. The spine should be very straight and the head tilted slightly forward with the chin tucked slightly in—the mind tends to be more restless when the head is raised too high. Reducing the amount of light in the room could also help, as bright light can stir up thoughts and feelings.

Patience is essential in dealing with a busy mind. Don't be upset with yourself if you can't keep your attention on the object of meditation. It takes time and persistent practice to learn to slow down and gain some control over the mind, so be easy on yourself.

Sleepiness and dullness

The very opposite of excitement is sleepiness. This can vary from a dull, listless state of mind to near-unconsciousness. It is related to another of our habits: usually, when we close our eyes and relax our mind and body, it's time to go to sleep!

First, make sure that your back is straight and your head is not bent forward too far. Open your eyes half-way and meditate with your gaze directed at the floor in front of you. Increasing the amount of light in the room should also help you to stay alert.

Another solution is to visualize your mind enclosed within a tiny seed in the central channel at the level of your navel, as before. This time, imagine that the seed shoots up the central channel and out through the crown of your head. The seed opens and your mind merges with vast, empty space. Concentrate on this experience for a while, then return to the meditation.

It is possible that sleepiness during meditation is symptomatic of underlying depression, in which case experimenting with some of the antidotes to depression on page 134 might help.

If your mind is still dull and sleepy after having tried these remedies, it would be best to either take a break—you can splash cold water on your face, get some fresh air, or do some stretching—or stop the meditation altogether and try again later.

Physical discomfort

Your meditations will flow smoothly if your body is relaxed and comfortable, but often it is difficult to get it into that state. Much of our physical tension is mind-related, arising from unresolved problems, fears, worries, or anger. The most effective solution is to recognize these problems and settle them in meditation. A short-term method for easing physical tension—to be used either at the beginning of a meditation session or during it—is to sweep the body with your attention. Start at the top of the head and travel downward through the body. Concentrate briefly on each part and consciously let it relax. Imagine that the tension simply dissolves.

Another method is to breathe deeply and slowly, and with much concentration imagine that the tension or pain leaves your body with each exhalation.

If neither of these methods works, you could try a more elaborate one: visualizing your body as hollow. Starting at the center of your chest, imagine that all the internal, solid parts of your body dissolve into light, and then into empty space. Everything within your chest, head, arms, and legs gradually dissolves and becomes empty. Your skin transforms into a very thin membrane of light to enclose this empty space. Concentrate for a while on this experience of your body being hollow, like a balloon.

If sitting causes discomfort or pain—in the knees or back, for example—it is all right to change to a more comfortable position. As meditation is an activity of the mind, not the body, it is more important to keep the mind clear and comfortable. However, at times it is useful just to *observe* the pain, which is a conscious experience, a mental perception, and try to overcome the usual fearful reaction to it. Instead of giving it the label "pain," see it as just a sensation, another type of energy. Doing such analysis should give you more insight into the workings of your mind and help you develop more control over your physical reactions.

An extension of this method of dealing with physical pain is mentally to increase it as much as possible. Imagine it getting worse and worse. After a while, return to the original pain—which now appears much less painful than before!

Another method is to visualize the suffering of all the beings of the universe and then, with great compassion, bring it mentally into the pain you are experiencing now. Think that you have taken on the pain of all beings, who are thus freed of all their suffering. Hold this thought and rejoice in it for as long as you can.

It is good to experiment with these methods for dealing with pain—but be careful not to overdo them and cause yourself an injury!

Noise

Although it is best to meditate in a quiet place, it's not always possible to find one. In the city we hear traffic, TVs and music, kids playing, people talking and yelling, airplanes passing overhead. But even out in the country or high in the mountains there are sounds: birds and animals, the wind blowing, a stream or river. It's unrealistic to think we can find a perfectly sound-free place to meditate, and it's mistaken to think that we can only meditate when there is no noise; rather it's a question of learning how to deal with it.

The problem is not so much the noise itself, but rather how our mind reacts to it. If the noise is pleasant, such as music we like, we feel attracted and want to pay attention to it rather than our object of meditation—that is *attachment*. If the noise is unpleasant, we feel irritation or *aversion*. Either way, we get stuck to the noise and it's difficult to let go of it and carry on with the meditation. Our mind starts making commentary about the noise: what it is, who's making it, recalling similar experiences in the past, thinking of trying to make it stop, and so on. It's these thoughts and feelings that are the problem.

The best way to deal with this situation is to recognize what is happening in your mind and learn to just be aware of the noise without reacting and making commentary on it. Realize that you can't stop the world from making noise just because you are meditating, but you can work on how your mind reacts. You might recall times when you were studying for an exam or engrossed in reading a really good book, and how you were oblivious to noise around you. You can learn to do the same while meditating.

One way to do this is to generate a strong, positive motivation at the beginning of your session (see page 20), so that you feel joyful and enthusiastic about meditating. Being half-hearted about meditation or seeing it as a chore makes it difficult to stay focused on the object.

Another useful technique is to make mental notes (see page 40) such as "noise" or "music" or "bird," then let go of them and bring your awareness back to your object of meditation. You can also make mental notes of whatever reactions you notice in your mind: "feeling attracted" or "feeling aversion," "thinking" or "remembering," then let go of these as well.

Working on your mind is the best solution, but it's OK to try to stop or reduce the noise if that doesn't cause problems for anyone. You can also arrange your schedule so that you meditate when things are more quiet, such as early in the morning, or wear ear plugs!

Strange images and sensations

Meditators sometimes experience unusual images appearing in the mind, or sensations such as the body expanding or shrinking, or the mind floating outside the body. These are normal reactions as the mind adjusts itself to new activity and nothing to worry about.

On the other hand, do not be attached to such experiences or try to repeat them—this will only distract you from the real purpose of meditation. Simply observe whatever images or feelings arise without clinging to or rejecting them, and let them disappear of their own accord.

However, if any disturbing experience occurs frequently and you are unable to free yourself from it, you should consult a meditation teacher or a more experienced practitioner. It might be best to discontinue your practice until you receive their advice.

Discouragement

We often hear people complain, "I can't meditate; I've tried but it doesn't work," or "I've been meditating for so many months but nothing is happening." However, the problem is usually that they are expecting too much too quickly.

We need to be realistic. Most of us have never in our lives tried to understand our mind or control our thoughts and feelings. Old habits are not easy to break. Even if the results of daily meditation don't appear for two or three years—although this is highly unlikely—it should not be a cause for worry or despair.

Positive changes do not appear suddenly out of the blue, but develop slowly, gradually, little by little every day, so be patient with yourself. Remember, just making an effort to understand and control the mind is meditation. If you are trying to do what is best for yourself and others, you can feel confident that your meditation is worthwhile.

Often, new meditators think that their negative minds are getting worse, not better! And they feel that it is meditation that has caused this. Consider, however, what happens when you wash clothes. When you first put them into water, a certain amount of dirt comes out. As you continue to scrub them the water gets dirtier and dirtier. You might even be surprised by the amount of dirt that they contained. It would be foolish to blame the soap, water and scrubbing for the dirt—the process of washing merely reveals what is there already, and is the right method for completely removing the dirt.

Similarly, meditation is the way to purify the mind of what is already there: at first we discover the gross negativities, then the more subtle ones.

So be patient and don't worry!

Part Three

MEDITATIONS ON THE MIND

1

Meditation on the Breath

As mentioned earlier, one kind of meditation, stabilizing meditation, is for the purpose of developing concentration. Concentration is a natural quality of our mind—we use it when we study, work, watch TV, or read a book. But our ability to concentrate is limited—our mind is easily distracted—and the things we concentrate on are not necessarily beneficial for ourselves and others. Concentration in itself is not positive—it depends on how we use it. A bank robber, for example, needs very good concentration to carry out his crime. As the goal of spiritual practice is freeing our minds from negative thoughts and emotions, and attaining perfect clarity, peace, and joy, we need to learn to concentrate our mind on positive, beneficial objects.

Stabilizing meditation involves focusing the mind on an object and bringing it back whenever it wanders away. Among the many objects recommended by the Buddha to use for developing concentration, the breath is one of the best. We are breathing all the time anyway, so we don't have to conjure up some object to focus our mind on. Also, as our breathing is happening right here, right now, focusing on it helps our mind stay in the present, the here-and-now, rather than getting lost in memories of the past or fantasies about the future. Following the breath with our attention has a naturally calming effect on our mind, thus quieting our normally busy thoughts. The fourteenth century Tibetan meditation master, Je Tsongkhapa, in his book *The Great Treatise on the Graduated Path to Enlightenment,* said that if you have a lot of discursiveness, you should definitely meditate on the breath.

There are several qualities of the mind that are essential in developing good concentration. One of these is mindfulness, or recollection, which enables us to remember a familiar object (like our breath) without forgetting it or wandering to other objects. Mindfulness also enables us to keep in mind what we're supposed to be doing while we are sitting there, and not to get completely spaced out!

Another essential quality is discriminating alertness, which, like a sentry, watches out for distractions. Alertness knows what's happening moment by moment—whether our mind is paying attention to the object of meditation, or has wandered off to something else. It is also able to recognize negative thoughts and emotions such as anger and desire, which disturb our mind and can lead to problems for ourselves and others. Developing the ability to recognize these when they arise in our mind and do something about them before they escalate helps us to avoid a lot of suffering.

Mindfulness and alertness are thus essential for successful meditation; and in our day-to-day lives they keep us centered, alert and conscientious, helping us to know what is happening in our mind *as it happens* and thus to deal skillfully with problems as they arise.

You can use the meditation on the breath either for your main practice or as a preliminary to other meditations. It is an invaluable technique: regular practice helps you gradually become more aware of your inner world, and gain more control over your mind. You will feel more relaxed and more able to enjoy life, having greater sensitivity to yourself and the people and things around you. And using your increased mindfulness in other meditations, you will be able to maintain your concentration for longer periods.

Meditation on the breath, and stabilizing meditation in general, is therefore important for both beginners and advanced meditators: for those who want a simple technique for relaxing and calming the mind and for serious meditators who devote their lives to spiritual development.

The practice

Begin by sitting in the seven-point posture (pages 24), or in whatever position is most comfortable for you. Relax all your muscles and the other parts of your body, while keeping your back straight. If there is any tension in any part of your body, let it dissolve and disappear. Let your breathing be natural so that your breath flows in and out in a natural rhythm.

Motivation Have a positive motivation for doing the meditation, for example, "I am going to meditate in order to generate in my mind more positive energy, and decrease the negative energy, for the benefit of myself and everyone else."

Decide how long you will meditate for (if you're a beginner, ten to thirty minutes is good; you can gradually increase the length of time as your concentration improves), and determine that for the duration of the session you will keep your attention on the breath in order to fulfill this purpose.

Now focus your mind on your breathing. You can do this either by focusing on the openings of your nostrils, where you can feel subtle sensations as the breath enters and leaves your body, or by focusing on the in-and-out movement of the abdomen with each breath.

Choose one of those two places, and keep your mind, your attention, on the sensations you can feel at that place during each inhalation and exhalation of your breath. Bring your mind back to this place every time it wanders away.

If you wish, you can count your breaths. You may find this helpful to keep your mind concentrated. You count each full inhalation and exhalation of the breath as one.

You can say to yourself, "Breathing in, breathing out, one. Breathing in, breathing out, two…" and so on. Count up to five or ten breaths, then start again at one. If your mind wanders in the middle of the counting, go back and start again at one. Continue counting in rounds of five or ten breaths, and bringing your attention back to the breath every time it wanders away. If your mind becomes more stable and is able to stay focused on the breath without needing to count, then you can dispense with the counting.

Don't try to control your breath; just breathe normally and gently. Inevitably, thoughts will appear, and your attention will be distracted by them, but as soon as you realize this has happened, bring your mind back to the breath.

Learn to have a neutral attitude toward your thoughts, being neither attracted nor repulsed. In other words, do not react with dislike, worry, excitement, or clinging to any thought, image, or feeling that arises. Merely notice its existence and return your attention to the breath. Even if you have to do this fifty times a minute, don't feel frustrated! Be patient and persistent; eventually your thoughts will subside.

It may be helpful to think that your mind is like the sky, and thoughts are like clouds. Clouds come and go in the sky—they do not stay long, nor do they alter the natural stillness and spaciousness of the sky. In the same way, thoughts come and go in the clear space of your mind; they are transient, momentary. If you can simply notice them and let them go, bringing your attention again and again to the breath, the thoughts will disappear on their own.

Be content to stay in the present. Accept whatever frame of mind you are in and whatever arises in your mind, without judging it as good or bad. Be free of expectation, clinging, and frustration. Have no wish to be somewhere else, to be doing something else, or even to feel some other way. Be content, just as you are.

When your skill has developed and your ability to avoid distractions has increased, you can take your alertness a step further. Make mental notes of the nature of the thoughts that arise, such as "thinking," "memory," "fantasy," "feeling angry," "attachment," "hearing a sound," "feeling bored," or "pain." As soon as you have noted the thought or feeling, let it go, recalling its impermanent nature.

Another technique is to use your distractions to help you gain insight into the nature of the mind. When a thought arises, instead of focusing on the thought itself, focus on the thinker. This means that one part of the mind, discriminating alertness, takes a look at another part, a distraction. The disturbing object will disappear, but hold your attention on the thinker for as long as you can. Again, when another thought comes, focus on the thinker and follow the same procedure. Return to watching the breath once the distractions have passed.

These methods for handling distractions can be applied to any meditation. It is no use ignoring or suppressing disturbing thoughts or negative energy, because they will recur persistently.

If a thought or feeling is particularly disturbing and you are unable to let go of it, you might need to take a short break from meditating on the breath and use one of the methods for dealing with negative energy on page 122. Once the disturbing emotion is more under control, you can return to focusing on the breathing.

Dedication When it's time to end the session, feel good about what you have done. Don't judge your meditation with thoughts such as, "that was a lousy meditation; my mind was all over the place." Remember that *just making the effort* to meditate is in itself very meaningful and beneficial. Rejoice in the positive energy you have generated, and dedicate it to the benefit of all beings—may their minds may become free from problems and unhappiness, and be filled instead with peace and joy.

2

Meditation on the Clarity of the Mind

The reality of our existence is that we are a combination of body and mind. Each of these in turn is a combination of many parts, all constantly in a state of flux. Unfortunately, our ego is not satisfied with such a simple explanation. It complicates matters by fabricating a view of an I or self based on our conceptions, likes, and dislikes. We think, "I'm attractive, " "I'm ugly," "I'm a good dancer, " "I won't succeed, " "I have a bad temper." We believe these projections and assume they are permanent and unchanging.

We do the same with people and objects in the world around us. We *believe* "he is ugly," "she is good." We build up our own elaborate and very solid picture of reality and hold on to it unquestioningly.

Meditation on the clarity of the mind is an effective antidote to our concrete projections. We can gain a direct experience of the clear, non-material, transient nature of all thoughts, feelings, and perceptions, thus weakening the tendency to identify with them. As the subject—the mind—softens, so too do its projected objects; they slowly lose their concreteness. The feeling of dislike toward the "bad person" may still arise through habit, but we have the space to recall, "This is a projection of my thought, which is clear and transitory. It rises like a wave in my mind and soon will pass. The object does not exist in the way I see it."

This meditation is especially effective for softening our view of our own self. Normally our self-esteem is low, based on past mistakes, personality faults, bad habits, and the like. But anger, jealousy, selfishness, depression and the other problems that haunt us are *mental* experiences and therefore clear and transitory. These states of mind *depend* for their existence on our belief in them! By recognizing this in meditation on the mind's nature we learn to let go of and stop identifying with these experiences.

Our intrinsic nature is clear and pure and is with us twenty-four hours a day. The negativities that rise and fall like waves on the ocean of our consciousness are temporary and can be eliminated. Consistent practice of this meditation will eventually generate a certainty about this pure nature to the point where it becomes our reality, our actual experience. This is a natural step toward understanding the more subtle nature of self and all phenomena: their emptiness of inherent existence (see page 53).

The practice

Motivation Have a positive motivation for doing the meditation.

Begin by breathing in deeply through both nostrils, bringing the air down to the stomach, holding it for a moment and then exhaling slowly and gently through your pursed lips. Repeat this two more times, then breathe normally in and out through your nose. Observe your breathing without thinking, without conceptualizing. Once your awareness has become sharp, turn your attention to the clarity of your consciousness.

Your consciousness, or mind, is whatever you are experiencing at the moment: sensations in your body, thoughts, feelings, perceptions of sounds, and so forth. The nature of each of these experiences is clarity, without form or color; space-like, pure awareness. Focus your attention on this clear, pure nature of the mind.

Initially it might be difficult to find the actual object, that is, the clarity. If so, meditate on a mental image of clarity—one way to generate such an image is to visualize space. Imagine lying on a hilltop and staring up at a sky that is completely clear and free of clouds. Concentrate on this vast, unobstructed emptiness. Imagine that it flows down and embraces you and your surroundings;

everything becomes empty like space. Hold this experience; feel that the nature of your mind is like this clear, empty space.

Thoughts and distractions will arise, but do not react to them; neither follow them nor reject them. Remember that they are clear by nature, without substance. Simply watch them come and go, then return to the awareness of the mind's clarity.

Do not think about anything during this meditation. There is no need to wonder what the mind is; simply *observe* it, its clear nature, which is like infinite, empty space. That is sufficient. Be natural. Meditation is simple and natural; it is nothing special.

Concentration means holding the mind on an object continuously, without forgetting it. The automatic result of concentration is awareness, which is free of concepts. A light does not need to think, "I am dispelling darkness"—it simply illuminates. Awareness is an inner light that enables us to see things more clearly. It dispels the heaviness of how things appear to us, thus weakening our clinging or aversion to them.

Meditate for short periods—ten to thirty minutes—until your concentration has improved. Then you can sit for an hour or more, or as long as you can maintain strong awareness. If the meditation is going well, you will feel light and relaxed.

Dedication Conclude the meditation session by dedicating the positive energy created during it to the happiness and welfare of everyone.

3
Meditation on the Continuity of the Mind

The mind has been compared to a vast ocean, and our perceptions, thoughts, and emotions to waves rising and falling on its surface. This analogy helps us to understand the experiences that occur while we are meditating or going about our daily activities. But to get a feeling for where the mind comes from and where it goes to, it is useful to think of it as a river, flowing through time.

Each moment of mind leads uninterruptedly to the next. The mind flows along ceaselessly, day and night, a stream of countless momentary experiences, always changing. Thoughts and feelings arise and quickly disappear, but they leave imprints that are carried on the mindstream.

Buddhism explains that the mind is without beginning or end, unlike the body, which is conceived, born, dies, and disintegrates. Our personality and experiences of this life are shaped by the imprints carried on the mind from past lives. Likewise, whatever we do and think now determines our future experiences (see the meditation on karma, page 80). It is up to us: we can be whatever we want as long as we channel our energies in that direction. To do this we need to understand the mind and learn how to use it skillfully.

Accepting the existence of other lives hinges on understanding the mind in this way. If you have been able to recall experiences from past lives you will realize that just as this life is the future of those past, so too will it be a past life of those to come. When your mind has become sufficiently calm you will be able to see deeply into it and realize it as an ever-flowing stream going far back in time. When you have experienced the reality of past lives for yourself, you will then be convinced of their existence.

However, for many people this is an alien idea. Here are several analytical approaches to considering the validity of mental continuity.

First, the mind is impermanent, transitory, changing from moment to moment. Thus it is an effect, a result—the product of causes and conditions. And the main cause of a mind is necessarily a previous moment of mind. Causes and their results must be the same type of phenomena, so it's not possible for mind, a non-physical phenomenon, to arise or be produced from a physical phenomenon such as the body, just as it's not possible for fire to be produced by water. Also, as mind is a series of ever-changing moments, each necessarily the result of a previous moment, how could it have a beginning in time?

Some people hold that the mind is the brain or activity in the brain. But as defined here, the mind is the experiences themselves—and how can thoughts and feelings be physical? If they were, scientists studying someone's brain should be able to see them, but that is not the case. They can know *when* the person is thinking, but not *what* they are thinking. The mind *depends* upon the brain and the nervous system, but cannot itself *be* the brain.

Nor can one's mind be derived from the minds of others, such as one's parents. Our body came into existence from parts of our parents' bodies, but our mind is a non-physical phenomenon, and arises in a completely different way. It's not possible for a part of one mind to break off and become a new mind. Also, if our mind *did* come from our parents' minds, then wouldn't we be born with all of their memories and knowledge?

This is clearly not the case. Our present personality, knowledge, and experiences are necessarily the result of our own past experiences and actions. Our mind, therefore, comes from its own previous continuity.

The meditation here is very helpful for experiencing our own mind as a continuously-flowing, ever-changing stream of events.

The practice

Motivation Sit comfortably and relax. Contemplate a positive, beneficial motivation for doing the meditation. Spend some time concentrating on your breath, until the mind is quiet and clear.

First, take a look at your present state of mind, at the thoughts and sensations flashing by. Just observe them in a detached way, without clinging to or rejecting any of them.

Now, start to travel backward through time. Briefly skim over the conscious experiences you have had since waking up this morning.... Are these part of the same stream of consciousness as your present experiences?

Before waking up, you were probably dreaming. Try to recall last night's dreams.... Do they also belong to this same mind-stream?

Continue to trace your mental experiences to yesterday, two days ago, last week, last month, last year; two, five, ten years ago. Continue to check if these experiences are of the same stream of consciousness.

Avoid getting involved in any of your recollections. The purpose of the meditation is not to relive good times or sort out problems from the past, but to get a feeling for the mind's continuity. If you should find something in your memory that you would like to investigate further, put it aside until later.

Go back in your life as far as you can, bringing to mind experiences from your adolescence and childhood.... People are sometimes able to remember their infancy, or even the time of birth. Relax and open your mind to allow such memories to arise....

If you have difficulty accessing memories from the early part of your life, don't worry. Realize that just as your present mindstream is the continuation of experiences that you *can* remember, those experiences in turn are the continuation of earlier ones that you can no longer remember.

Now, think of your birth, the time you were in the womb, and the moment of your conception. If your mind is a stream of experiences, each one arising from the one before it, then did it exist throughout these experiences, or did it begin to exist at some point? Consider the different possibilities: did it arise from your parents' minds? If so, when and how?… Or did it arise out of nowhere, without any causes and conditions?… Or did it arise from a mindstream that already existed before you were conceived, in another life?… See if you can open your mind to that possibility. You might even be able to glimpse a memory from another life….

Having reached back into your memory as far as you can, now gently bring your awareness into the present and again observe the thoughts and feelings that arise. Simply experience your stream of consciousness as it continues to flow; feel its momentum: one thought or feeling leading to the next, which leads to the next, which leads to the next, on and on.

Finally, try to get some idea of where it goes from here. Contemplate your mindstream flowing through the rest of the day, and then tomorrow, the coming days, weeks and years...up until death. What happens then?

Consider the different possibilities: does the stream of consciousness suddenly cease to exist? Does it transform into something else? Does it continue on, encountering new experiences?

Consider these possibilities carefully, using the reasons given earlier. Although you might not come to any definite conclusion, the important thing is to look with a clear and open mind.

Dedication Finally, dedicate any insight you have gained to your eventual understanding of your mind for the sake of all living beings.

Part Four

ANALYTICAL
MEDITATIONS

About Analytical Meditation

The meditations presented here are solutions to a wide variety of problems and will help you develop a more realistic view of your inner and outer worlds.

A meditation on emptiness is given first, as this is the most powerful remedy to any difficulty. It has us investigate our sense of a solid, permanent, independent "I," which lies at the root of all our problems. However, emptiness is a very difficult concept and you may find this meditation too challenging to begin with, so you might want to just read through it, then go back to it later after you have more experience with the other meditations. But even to start questioning what we have always believed to be true about our existence is very worthwhile.

The other meditations get us to look at our assumptions about life, suffering, death, love, and human relationships and to see that it is these assumptions and their attendant expectations that cause our unhappiness and frustrations.

The section on dealing with negative energy gives advice on how to handle problems as they occur in day-to-day life.

Begin the meditations with a few minutes—or as long as you like—of meditation on the breath, slowing down the mind and observing its present state.

Then, start the analysis. Do not let your mind wander from the subject you are analyzing: the more concentrated you are, the more effective your meditation will be. Dissolve your mind in the subject, penetrating it with intellectual thought, questions, images, and illustrations from your own experience. Your meditation might take the form of an internal lecture, as though you were explaining a point to yourself; a debate, with yourself taking both sides; or a freestyle thought-adventure.

Doubts may arise, but do not gloss over them. Doubts are questions and questions need answers, so be clear about what you think, and why. Either come to a conclusion about the point in question or leave it aside for the moment and tackle it again later. If you are unable to resolve your doubts on your own, it's best to consult a teacher or more experienced student of this tradition.

If during the analysis you should develop an intuitive experience of the subject, stop analyzing and hold the feeling with single-pointed concentration for as long as possible. When the feeling fades, resume the investigation or conclude the session. This union of analytical and stabilizing meditations is essential if we are to achieve true mind-transformation. In analytical meditation we think about and understand intellectually a particular point, and through stabilizing meditation we gradually make it a part of our very experience of life.

1

Meditation on Emptiness

All Buddhist teachings are for the purpose of leading one gradually to the realization of emptiness. Here, *emptiness* means the emptiness of inherent, concrete existence; and the total eradication from our mind of this false way of seeing things marks our achievement of enlightenment, buddhahood.

What *is* "emptiness of inherent existence"? In practical terms, what does it mean? So-called inherent existence—which all things are said to lack, to be empty of—is a quality that we instinctively project onto every person and everything we experience. We see things as fully, solidly existing in and of themselves, from their own side, having their own nature, quite independent of causes, conditions, parts, or our own mind experiencing them.

Take a table, for example. We see a solid, independent table standing there, and it's so obviously a table that it seems ridiculous to even question it. But where is the table? Imagine taking it apart and laying the pieces out on the ground. Now see if you can find the table: is it one of the legs? Or its top? Is it the glue or nails that hold it together? Or even one of its atoms?

If you investigate thoroughly, you will discover that you simply cannot find the table you think is there. That does not mean there is no table at all. There *is* a dependently-existing, changing-from-moment-to-moment table—the "table" that we merely label onto its parts—but this is not what we see. This is the crux of the problem. We experience not the bare reality of each thing and each person but an exaggerated, filled-out image of it projected by our own mind. This mistake marks every one of our mental experiences, is quite instinctive and is the very root of all our problems.

This pervasive mental disorder starts with the misapprehension of our own self. We are a composite of body—a mass of flesh, bones, skin, cells, and atoms—and mind—a stream of thoughts, feelings, and perceptions. This composite is conveniently known as "Mary," "Harold," "woman," or "man." It is a temporary alliance that ends with the death of the body and the flowing on of the mind to other experiences.

These stark, unembellished facts can be rather disquieting. A part of us, the ego, craving security and immortality, invents an inherent, independent, permanent self. This is not a deliberate, conscious process but one that takes place deep in our subconscious mind.

This fantasized self appears especially strongly at times of stress, excitement or fear. For example, when we narrowly escape an accident there is a powerful sense of an I that nearly suffered death or pain and must be protected. That I does not exist; it is a hallucination.

Our adherence to this false I—known as self-grasping ignorance—taints all our dealings with the world. We are attracted to people, places, and situations that gratify and uphold our self-image, and react with fear or animosity to whatever threatens it. We view all people and things as definitely this way or that. Thus this root, self-grasping, branches out into attachment, jealousy, anger, arrogance, depression, and the myriad other turbulent and unhappy states of mind.

The final solution is to eliminate this root ignorance—with the wisdom that realizes the emptiness, in everything we experience, of the false qualities we project onto things. This is the ultimate transformation of mind.

Emptiness sounds pretty abstract but in fact is very practical and relevant to our lives. The first step toward understanding it is to try and get an idea of what it is we *think* exists; to locate, for example, the I that we believe in so strongly and then, by using clear reasoning in analytical meditation, to see that it is a mere fabrication, something that has never existed and could never exist in the first place.

But don't throw out too much! You definitely exist! There is a conventional, interdependent self that experiences happiness and suffering, that works, studies, eats, sleeps, meditates, and becomes enlightened. The first, most difficult task is to distinguish between this valid I and the fabricated one; usually we cannot tell them apart. In the concentration of meditation it is possible to see the difference; to recognize the illusory I and eradicate our long-habituated belief in it. The meditation here is a practical first step in that direction.

The practice

Motivation Begin with a meditation on the breath to relax and calm your mind. Motivate yourself strongly to do this meditation in order to finally become enlightened for the sake of all beings.

Now, with the alertness of a spy, slowly and carefully become aware of the I. Who or what is it that thinks, feels, and meditates? How does it appear to you? Is your I a creation of your mind? Or is it something that exists concretely and independently, in its own right?

Now, try to locate it. Where is this I? Is it in your head ... in your eyes ... in your heart ... in your hands ... in your stomach ... in your feet? Carefully consider each part of your body, including the organs, blood vessels, and nerves. Can you find your I? It might be very small and subtle, so consider the cells, the atoms, the sub-atomic particles.

If you do think that your I is a part of the body, then what would happen if that part were removed in an operation, or damaged in an accident? And what happens to the I when your body ceases to function at death?

Perhaps you think your mind is the I. The mind is a constantly changing stream of thoughts, feelings, and other experiences, coming and going in rapid succession. It's never the same from one moment to the next. Which of these experiences is the I? Is it a loving thought ... an angry thought ... a happy feeling ... a depressed feeling?

If you think that your I *is* one of these experiences, then what happens to it when that kind of experience is not present in your mind? If your I is love, for example, then when your mind is filled only with anger, does the I go somewhere else, or disappear altogether? Is there no I at that time? Or maybe you have many "I"s: an angry one, a loving one, a frightened one, etc.?

If you cannot find the I in your body or your mind, then could it be something else? Is there some extra part of you other than your body and mind? After all, we say "my body" and "my mind," implying the existence of something else that owns these two. If so, what is it? Where is it found? What kind of phenomenon is it? Examine every possibility you can think of.

Again, look at the way your I actually appears, how it feels to you. After this search for the I, do you notice any change? Do you still believe that it is as solid and real as you felt before? Does it still appear to exist independently, in and of itself?

Next, mentally disintegrate your body. Imagine all the atoms separating and floating apart. Billions and billions of minute particles scatter throughout space. Imagine that you can actually see this.

Now, disintegrate your mind. Let every thought, feeling, sensation and perception float away.... Then check your feeling of I—where is it? What is it?

Do not make the mistake of thinking, "My body is not the I and my mind is not the I, therefore I don't exist." You *do* exist, but not in the way you instinctively feel: as something independent and inherent. Conventionally, your self exists *in dependence upon* mind and body, and this combination is the basis to which conceptual thinking ascribes a name: "I" or "self" or "Mary" or "Harold." This is the you that is sitting and meditating and wondering, "Do I exist?"

Whatever exists is necessarily dependent upon causes and conditions, or parts and names, for its existence. A car, for example, is a collection of pieces of steel, glass, plastic, rubber, an engine, etc., put together by people in a factory. We give the name "car" to this collection, but if we look for a real, concrete, independently existing car, it cannot be found.

So conventionally things exist dependently, and understanding dependence is the principal cause for understanding their ultimate nature, emptiness. The conventional nature of an object is its dependence upon other things, and its ultimate nature is its emptiness of inherent, independent existence.

Think now about how your body exists conventionally: *in dependence upon* skin, blood, bones, legs, arms, organs and so forth. In turn, each of these exists *in dependence upon* their own parts: cells, atoms, and sub-atomic particles.

Think about your mind, how it exists *in dependence upon* thoughts, feelings, perceptions, sensations. And how, in turn, each of these exists *in dependence upon* the previous conscious experiences that gave rise to it.

Now, go back to your feeling of self or I. Think about how you exist conventionally, *in dependence upon* mind and body and name—the self's parts.

When the body feels hungry or cold, for example, you think "I am hungry," "I am cold." When the mind has an idea about something, you say "I think." When you feel love for someone you say "I love you." When introducing yourself, you say "I am so-and-so."

Apart from this sense of I that depends upon the ever-flowing, ever-changing streams of body and mind, is there an I that is solid, unchanging, and independent?

The mere absence of such an inherently-existing I is the emptiness of the self.

Dedication Finish the session with a conclusion as to how you, your *self*, exists. Conclude by dedicating sincerely any positive energy and insight you have gained to the enlightenment of all beings. Think that this meditation is just one step along the path to finally achieving direct insight into emptiness and thus cutting the root of suffering and dissatisfaction.

2
Appreciating our Human Life

The function of analytical meditation is to help us recognize and cut through the mistaken attitudes and ideas that cause unhappiness and dissatisfaction. Our experiences in life depend upon how we think and feel about things, and because most of the time we do not perceive things the way they really are, we encounter one frustrating situation after another.

As long as we blame our parents, society, or other external factors, we will never find any satisfying solutions to our problems. Their main cause lies within our own mind, so we need to take responsibility for changing our way of thinking where it is mistaken, that is, where it brings unhappiness to ourselves and others.

This can be done through meditation, by gradually becoming aware of how we think and feel, distinguishing correct from incorrect attitudes, and finally counteracting harmful attitudes by the appropriate means.

The starting point for many problems is the way we feel about ourselves and our life. Human existence is very precious, but normally we fail to appreciate it. We have so much potential, so much latent wisdom and loving kindness, so much to offer the world, but we may ignore or be unaware of this and let ourselves become clouded with depression. Focusing on shortcomings in our character and failings in our dealings with people and work, for example, or the harm we may have done to others, we develop an unfair, low opinion of ourselves. This self-image becomes more and more concrete with time. We identify ourselves as incapable and inadequate and feel hopeless and depressed. Or we turn to other people in an attempt to find happiness and fulfillment. However, as our friends are likely to feel the same way about themselves, such relationships often bring only more frustration.

We can unlock the potential for happiness and satisfaction that lies within every one of us by becoming aware of our mental processes, and then applying discriminating wisdom to all our actions of body, speech, and mind. But to hope to be able to achieve this, and, through it, fulfillment, without first completing the necessary groundwork is to invite frustration. We must start by building a firm foundation, based on a realistic view of ourselves. We have to accept our positive as well as our negative traits, and determine to nourish the good and transform or eliminate the bad aspects of our character. Eventually we will recognize how fortunate we are to have been born human. Once we understand this, we can begin to train our minds to achieve enlightenment.

When we look at ourselves deeply, carefully, we find that most of our day-to-day problems are quite trivial. It is only our projections and conceptions that complicate them and allow them to grow out of all proportion. As we self-indulgently become caught up in our problems, they appear to grow larger and larger, and we disappear into deep states of depression and hopelessness. Wallowing in self-pity, we are unable to see that, in fact, we have created our problems and, therefore, our depressive state.

This meditation is an antidote to negative states of being such as depression and hopelessness. It helps us to recognize and rejoice in our good fortune, in our extraordinary and unique potential to achieve true happiness and satisfaction. An understanding of this potential naturally fills us with joy and enthusiasm for life—who wouldn't feel elated at the realization that they hold the key to their own fulfillment? At the same time, recognizing our good fortune helps us to see clearly that there are many who are infinitely less fortunate than we are. We feel true compassion for them and take an active concern in their plight.

The practice

Sit comfortably with your back straight. Relax your body and let any tension dissolve and flow away.... Spend a few minutes calming and settling your mind using the meditation on the breath (page 37) or the nine-round breathing practice (page 28).

Motivation When your mind is calm and settled in the here-and-now, generate a positive, altruistic motivation for doing the meditation. You can think, for example, "May this meditation bring greater peace and happiness to myself and others, to the whole world," or "May this meditation bring me closer to enlightenment so that I can help all other beings attain enlightenment as well."

Begin the meditation by contemplating that the nature of your mind is clear and pure, and has the potential to become enlightened: the state of complete purity, goodness, and perfection. This is true for yourself and all other beings. You can think, for example, "The nature of every being's mind is clear like space, vast, and unlimited. Our negative thoughts and emotions are not permanent, fixed parts of the mind, but are transient, like clouds that pass through the sky. And because they are based on ignorance and misconceptions, they can be cleared away and the mind can be developed to a state that is completely pure and positive."

Alternatively, if you find it difficult to accept that the mind has the potential to become enlightened, you can think of the positive qualities that you have—intelligence, loving-kindness, compassion, generosity, courage, etc.—and remind yourself that these can be developed even further, and that you can use your life to bring benefit and happiness to others.

Spend some time contemplating this, and feel joyful about the potential that lies within you.

Although all beings have the potential to transform their mind and become enlightened, not all beings are in the most ideal situation in which they can recognize and develop this potential. Human beings are generally in the best situation. Non-human beings either have too much suffering or are incapable of developing their potential due to ignorance and other delusions.

Imagine what it would be like as an animal, for example. Animals in the wild have no one to care for them when they experience hunger, thirst, heat, cold, sickness, or injuries, and are in almost constant fear for their lives. Domestic animals are sometimes better off, but lack freedom and are often killed for meat, fur, or other products. And all animals, even the most intelligent, have extremely limited mental capacities and are unable to develop themselves intellectually or spiritually. Contemplate this to get a sense of how fortunate you are to have a human life.

However, not all human beings have the right conditions to recognize and develop their potential. Imagine, for example, being a destitute beggar, or living in a war zone. Most of your time and energy would be spent simply trying to keep yourself and your family alive; you would have little or no time to think of anything else such as spiritual practice.

Imagine suffering from a severe mental disability or illness, which would make it very difficult for you to understand the teachings on the mind's potential and how to develop it. Or having a physical condition that caused you a great deal of pain, discomfort, and inconvenience, and hindered your ability to learn and practice spiritual teachings.

Some people do not have access to spiritual teachings that explain the mind's potential and how to develop it. Imagine spending your entire life in a small, remote village where no one has even heard about enlightenment, so there's no opportunity to learn how to attain it.

Other people may be aware of their potential and sincerely wish to practice the teachings on how to develop it, but are prevented from doing so by others. For example, people in some countries do not have freedom of religion; others face strong objections from their parents, spouse, or children. Imagine yourself in such a situation, recognize how difficult it would be, and appreciate the freedom that you have.

Then, there are many people who are physically and mentally healthy, are materially well-off and have the freedom and opportunity to learn spiritual teachings, but are simply not interested. Their interests lie elsewhere: accumulating wealth, property, and possessions, acquiring worldly knowledge or skills, or in simply experiencing as much pleasure as they can. They never consider that all these things will be left behind when they die—like a dream that vanishes as soon as we wake up—and that only their mind will continue to the next life.

Some people engage in harmful actions such as killing, stealing, being abusive or dishonest, not realizing that these actions cause suffering to themselves and others, and create further obstacles to discovering their true potential. Recognize how fortunate you are to be interested in enlightenment and using your life in meaningful, beneficial ways, for yourself and others.

Now bring to mind the positive qualities and advantages you have. You are a human being with an intelligent mind, a loving heart, and a body you can put to good use. There are people who care about and support you—family, friends, a spiritual teacher. You have opportunities to pursue your creative, intellectual, and social interests. You enjoy a good standard of living—at least, you have enough to stay alive! And most of all, you have the potential and opportunity—*because* of all the other benefits—to investigate, understand, and transform your mind.

Even if your life does not afford as much freedom and comfort as you would like, and even if you have to live with some very difficult problems and challenges, no matter where you are and what conditions you live in, you can always work on your mind.

Think now how few people or creatures on earth share these freedoms and chances with you. When you have considered this deeply, you will realize how rare and precious a life like yours is. Really appreciate your good fortune.

Once you have seen the disadvantages your life is free of and the advantages you enjoy, decide how best to use your precious opportunities. Think of all the possibilities open to you—work, travel, enjoyment, study. If you wish to offer service to others, there are countless opportunities to help those less fortunate than you. But the most meaningful and beneficial thing you can do, both for yourself and others, is to develop yourself spiritually: overcoming the negative aspects of your mind and increasing the positive, and actualizing your potential for enlightenment.

Try to see the limitations of a lifestyle geared solely to materialistic gain. Think of the insignificance of fame, wealth, reputation, and sensual indulgence when compared to the goal of enlightenment. Why aspire to only temporal achievements when we are capable of so much more?

See if you can feel a sense of joy and appreciation for the wonderful situation you have. Resolve to use your life wisely—doing your best to avoid harming others, and instead helping them as much as you can, and developing your love, compassion, wisdom, and other positive qualities that will enable you to actualize your highest potential.

Dedication Finally, dedicate the energy and inspiration you have gained from doing this meditation to the ultimate happiness of all beings.

3
Meditation on Impermanence

Everything in the physical world is impermanent, changing all the time. Some changes are obvious: people grow up, get old, and die; buildings and bridges wear out and fall apart. The environment goes through a complete transformation from one season to the next; flowers wilt, paint cracks and peels, cars break down.

The source of this external transformation can be traced to the cellular and molecular composition of matter, where change is not so obvious. At this invisible level, minute particles are constantly coming into or going out of existence, gathering and dispersing, expanding and contracting—always in motion, always fluctuating.

Our conscious world is also changing constantly. Sometimes we are happy, sometimes depressed; sometimes we feel full of love, other times full of anger. Memories of conversations and events, thoughts of the future, ideas about this and that fill our minds one after the other. A few moments of looking inward will show us how quickly the mind is changing: it's like a railway station at rush hour! Streams of thoughts, feelings, and perceptions flash by, in every direction, without ceasing.

This constant change is the reality of things, but we find it very difficult to accept. Intellectually, it is not a problem; but real acceptance of impermanence rarely, if ever, enters our everyday behavior and experience. Instinctively, we cling to people and things as if they were permanent and unchanging. We don't want the nice person or the beautiful object to change, and firmly believe that the irritating person will never be different. And when we are depressed or dissatisfied, we think we will be that way forever.

We cling especially strongly to our view of our own personality: "I am a depressed person," "I am an angry person," "I am not very intelligent." We might indeed be this or that, but it is not the whole picture nor will it always be like that; it will change.

By not recognizing impermanence we meet with frustration, irritation, grief, loneliness, and countless other problems. We can avoid experiencing them by becoming familiar with the transitory nature of things, recognizing that they are in a constant state of flux. Gradually we will learn to expect, and accept, change as the nature of life.

We will understand not only that change simply happens but also that we can bring about change. We have the power to change what we are, to develop and transform our minds and lives.

The practice

Motivation Sit comfortably and relax completely. Take time to calm and concentrate your thoughts by mindfully observing the breath. When your mind is calm and settled in the present, generate a positive motivation for doing the meditation. For example, you can think: "May this meditation help bring about greater peace and happiness for all beings," or: "May this meditation be a cause for me to become enlightened so that I can help all beings become free of suffering and become enlightened as well."

Then, turn your awareness to your body. Think of its many different parts—arms, legs, head, skin, blood, bones, nerves, and muscles. Examine them, one by one; *probe* them with your feelings. Contemplate the nature of these things: their substance, their texture, their shape and size. Be sensitive to the body at work, the movement that is occurring every moment: the ebb and flow of your breath, the beating of your heart, the flow of your blood, and the energy of your nerve impulses.

Be aware of your body at the even more subtle level of its cellular structure, that it is entirely composed of living cells coming into existence, moving about, reproducing, dying, and disintegrating.

On an even subtler level, all the parts of your body are made of molecules, atoms, and sub-atomic particles, and these are in constant motion. Try to really get a feeling for the change that is taking place every moment in your body....

Now, turn your attention to your mind. It, too, is composed of many parts: thoughts, perceptions, feelings, memories, and images following one after the other, ceaselessly. Spend a few minutes simply observing the ever-changing flow of experiences in your mind, like someone looking out of a window onto a busy street, watching the cars and pedestrians passing by. Don't cling to anything that you see in your mind, don't judge or make comments—just observe, and try to get a sense of the impermanent, ever-changing nature of your mind.

After reflecting on the impermanence of your inner world—your own body and mind—extend your awareness to the outer world. Think about your immediate surroundings: the cushion, mat, or bed you are sitting on, the floor, walls, windows, and ceiling of your room, the furniture and other objects in the room. Consider that each of these, although appearing solid and static, is actually a mass of tiny particles whizzing around. Stay with that experience for a while.

Then let your awareness travel further out, beyond the walls of your room. Think of other people: their bodies and minds are also constantly changing, not staying the same for even one moment. The same is true of all living beings, such as animals, birds, and insects.

Think of all the inanimate objects in the world and in the universe: houses, buildings, roads, cars, trees, mountains, oceans and rivers, the earth itself, the sun, moon, and stars. All of these things, being composed of atoms and other minute particles, are constantly changing, every moment, every millisecond. Nothing stays the same without changing. Concentrate on this experience.

During the meditation, any time that you have a clear, strong feeling of the ever-changing nature of things, hold your attention firmly on it for as long as possible without letting your mind be distracted (in other words, do stabilizing meditation). Soak your mind in the experience. When the feeling fades or your attention starts to wander, again analyze the impermanence of either your body or mind or another object.

Conclude the meditation with the thought that it is unrealistic and self-defeating to cling to things as though they were permanent. Whatever is beautiful and pleasing will change and eventually disappear, so we can't expect it to give us lasting happiness. Also, whatever is unpleasant or disturbing won't last forever—it might even change for the better! So there's no need to be upset, or to reject it.

Dedication Dedicate your positive energy and insight to the happiness of all living beings.

4

Death Awareness
Meditation

When first confronted with the idea of meditating on death we might react with shock. Perhaps we think that meditation should deal with good experiences, whereas death and things associated with it—tears of grief, black clothing, skeletons, and cemeteries—evoke feelings of fear and panic. We see death as the contradiction of life, beauty, and happiness; it belongs to the realm of the unmentionable, the unthinkable.

But why do we have such unrealistic attitudes? Why are we unable to accept death as calmly as we accept yesterday's fresh flowers wilting today? Change, disintegration, and death are natural, inevitable aspects of existence.

Buddhism explains death as the separation of mind and body, after which the body disintegrates and the mind continues to another life. The conventional self or I that depends on the present mind-body combination ends at death, but a different self-image will arise with the new life. Death is therefore not a cessation but a transition, a transformation.

At the root of our uneasiness and denial is ignorance. We cling to our self-image as something permanent and unchanging, and want it to live forever. This wish may not be conscious, expressible in thoughts or words, but it is definitely there; it accounts for why we instinctively flee, struggle, or shield ourselves when our life is threatened.

This is not to imply that there is something wrong with trying to stay alive—life is indeed very precious. But it would be useful to examine the nature of the I that does not want to die. The fault is not in the wish to prolong life but in the fundamental idea of who or what we really are. "Am I the body, or any part of this collection of bones, blood, and flesh?" "Am I my consciousness?" "Am I something other than my body and my mind?"

The understanding of emptiness, or the non-existence of an inherent, permanent self, frees us from fear of death and from *all* fears and misconceptions. Until that point is reached, however, it is important to maintain awareness of impermanence and death.

The principal benefit of practicing this meditation is that it forces us to decide what attitudes and activities are truly worthwhile. Human life is highly significant because of the opportunities it provides for our spiritual growth: developing love and compassion, clarity and wisdom, and finally achieving enlightenment. Every one of us has this potential.

But life is short. Death can happen at any time, and to die without having undertaken the only work that has any lasting benefit, either to ourselves or to others, would be highly regrettable. The present life and all its experiences are fleeting; clinging to anything in this world is like chasing a rainbow. If we keep this in mind constantly we will not waste time on mundane pursuits but spend it wisely, avoiding what is negative and thus the cause of unhappiness, and cultivating what is positive and thus the cause of happiness.

How we live our life inevitably affects how we die. If we live peacefully, we will die with peace; but if we fail to take death into consideration and thus fail to prepare for it, we are likely to die with fear and regret—states of mind that will only compound our suffering.

There is no need whatsoever to regard death with fear or sorrow. It can in fact be an enlightening experience, but whether or not it will be depends on how we live every day, every moment of our life. Awareness of death during life helps us to stay in the present, to see the past as dream-like and hopes for the future as fantasies.

We will be more stable and content and will enthusiastically make the most of our life.

There are various ways of meditating on death; the one explained here involves contemplating nine points. The nine points are subsumed under three main points:

- The inevitability of death
- The uncertainty of the time of death
- The fact that only spiritual insight can help you at the time of death

There are different ways you can meditate on the nine points. One way is to meditate on all nine points in one session; another is to do one point per session, thus taking nine sessions to complete all the points. A third alternative is to spend one session on each of the three main points with its three sub-points. Feel free to choose whichever way you find most helpful.

The practice

As preparation, sit in a comfortable position, with your back straight, and let your body relax. Spend some time letting your mind settle down in the present moment; let go of thoughts of the past and the future. Make the decision to keep your mind focused on the meditation topic for the duration of the meditation session.

Motivation When your mind is calm and settled in the present, generate a positive motivation for doing the meditation. For example, you can think: "May this meditation help bring about greater peace and happiness for all beings," or: "May this meditation be a cause for me to become enlightened so that I can help all beings become free of suffering and become enlightened as well." You might like to recite some of the prayers on pages 171–74.

Then, with your mind relaxed but fully concentrated, contemplate the following points, bringing in your own experiences and insights, as well as things you have heard or read. Try to feel every point deeply. Remember, if at any time during the session you reach a strong, intuitive experience of the point you are examining, hold the feeling with your attention as long as possible.

The inevitability of death

We plan many activities and projects for the coming days, months, and years. Although death is the only event that is certain to occur, we don't usually think about it or plan for it. Even if the thought of death does arise in our mind, we usually push it away quickly—we don't want to think about death. But it's important to think about and be prepared for it. Contemplate the following three points to get a sense that death is definitely going to happen to you.

1. Everyone has to die

To generate an experience of death's inevitability, first bring to mind people from the past: famous rulers and writers, musicians, philosophers, saints, scientists, criminals, and ordinary people. These people were once alive—they worked, thought, and wrote; they loved and fought, enjoyed life and suffered. And finally they died.

Is there anyone who ever lived who did not have to die? No matter how wise, wealthy, powerful, or popular a person may be, his or her life must come to an end. The same is true for all other living creatures. For all the advances in science and medicine, no one has found a cure for death, and no one ever will.

Now bring to mind people you know who have already died.... And think of the people you know who are still alive. Contemplate that every one of these people will die. And so will you.

There are several billion people on the planet right now, but one hundred years from now, all these people—with the exception of a few who are now very young—will be gone. You yourself will be dead. Try to experience this fact with your entire being.

2. Your lifespan is decreasing continuously

Time never stands still—it is continuously passing. Seconds become minutes, minutes become hours, hours become days,

days become years, and as time is passing in this way, you travel closer and closer toward death. Imagine an hour-glass, with the sand running into the bottom. The time you have to live is like the grains of sand, continuously running out…. Hold your awareness for a while on the experience of this uninterrupted flow of time carrying you to the end of your life.

If you were to fall from an airplane without a parachute you would be fully aware of death's approach. Imagine this is actually happening to you, and check what thoughts and feelings pass through your mind.

The reality of your situation in life is not so different: you are constantly moving toward death and can do nothing to avoid or postpone it.

3. The amount of time spent during your life to develop your mind is very small

Given that the mind alone continues after death, the only thing that will be of any value when you die is the positive and constructive energy you have created during your life. But how much time do you actually devote to understanding your mind, being kind to others, developing wisdom and compassion?

In an average day, how many hours do you sleep? How many hours do you work? How many hours do you spend preparing food, eating, socializing? How much time do you spend feeling depressed, frustrated, bored, angry, resentful, jealous, lazy, or critical? And finally, how much time do you spend consciously trying to improve your state of mind?

Do these calculations honestly. Assess your life in this practical way to see clearly just how much of your time is spent doing things that truly benefit yourself and others and that will be helpful for your mind at the time of death and in the next life.

By meditating on these first three points, you should be able to develop the determination to use your life wisely and mindfully.

The uncertainty of the time of death

By contemplating the first three points, you come to accept that you are definitely going to die. But you might think that death is not going to happen for a long time. Why do you think this way? Is there any way you can know for sure when death will happen? Contemplate the following three points to get a sense of how the time of death is completely uncertain and unknown.

4. Human life-expectancy is uncertain

If human beings died at a specific age, say eighty-eight, we would have plenty of time and space to prepare for death. But there is no such certainty, and death catches most of us by surprise.

Life can end at any point: at birth, in childhood, in adolescence, at the age of twenty-two or thirty-five or fifty or ninety-four. Think of examples of people you knew or have heard of who died before they reached the age you are now at....

Being young and healthy is no guarantee that a person will live a long time—children sometimes die before their parents. Healthy people can die before those who are suffering from a terminal illness such as cancer.... We can *hope* to live until we are seventy or eighty, but we cannot be certain of doing so. We cannot be certain that we will not die later today.

It is very difficult to feel convinced that death could happen at any moment. We tend to feel that since we've survived so far, our continuation is secure. But thousands of people die every day and few of them expected to.

Generate a strong feeling of the complete uncertainty of your own time of death; how there simply is no guarantee that you have long to live.

5. There are many causes of death

There are many different ways that death happens to people. Sometimes it happens due to external causes. These include natural disasters such as earthquakes, floods, and volcanic eruptions, or accidents such as car or plane crashes. People can also be killed by other people—murderers or terrorists—or by dangerous animals or poisonous insects.

Death can also happen due to internal causes. There are hundreds of different diseases that can rob us of our health and lead to death. There are also cases of people who are not ill, but something goes wrong in their bodies and they suddenly die, in their sleep or while walking around. And then there is old age; no one is safe from that. Even things that normally support life can become the cause of death. Food, for example, is something we need in order to stay alive, but it can sometimes lead to death, as when people overeat or eat contaminated food. Medicine normally supports life, but people sometimes die because they took the wrong medicine, or the wrong dose. Houses and apartments enable us to live comfortably, but they sometimes catch fire or collapse, killing the people inside.

People die in their sleep, in the womb, coming home from work, going to school, on the playing field, cooking dinner. Death can occur at any time, in any situation. Bring to mind cases of people you know or have heard of who have died, and think of *how* they died. Think that any of these things could happen to you as well.

6. The human body is very fragile

Our human body is very vulnerable; it can be injured or struck down by illness so easily. Within minutes, it can change from being strong and active to being helplessly weak and full of pain.

Right now you might feel healthy, energetic, and secure, but something as small as a virus or as insignificant as a thorn could drain your strength and lead to your death.

Think about this. Recall the times you have hurt or injured your body, and how easily it could happen again and even cause your death.

Your body won't last forever. In the course of your life you might manage to avoid illness and accidents, but the years will eventually overtake you—your body will degenerate, lose its beauty and vitality, and finally die.

By meditating on this second set of three points we will develop the determination to begin our work of mind-transformation right now, as the future is so uncertain.

The fact that only spiritual insight can help you at the time of death

No matter how much we have acquired or developed throughout our life—in terms of family and friends, wealth, power, travel, experiences, and so on—none of it goes with us at death. Only our stream of consciousness continues, carrying imprints of all that we have thought, felt, said, and done. It is vital that when we die we have as many positive imprints—the cause of good experiences— and as few negative imprints—the cause of suffering—on our mind as possible. Also, we should aim to die at peace with ourselves, feeling good about how we lived our life, and not leaving behind any unresolved conflicts with people.

The only things that will truly benefit us at the time of death are positive states of mind such as faith (see page 167), non-attachment and calm acceptance of the changes that are taking place, loving-kindness, compassion, patience, and wisdom. But in order to be able to have such states of mind at the time of death, we need to make ourselves familiar with them during the course of our life—and this is the essence of spiritual practice. Realizing this will give us the incentive to start doing spiritual practice now, and to practice as much as we can while we still have time.

You can experience a strong feeling of this reality by contemplating the following three points while visualizing yourself actually dying.

7. Your loved ones cannot help

When you face difficult or frightening situations, your thoughts usually turn to loved ones: your family and friends. So it is natural that you would wish them to be with you when you die. However, it's not certain that they will be there—you might die far from home.

But even if they were present with you at the time of death, would they be able to help you? Although they love you very much and do not want you to die, they cannot prevent this from happening. Also, chances are that they wouldn't know what to say or do to give you peace of mind; instead, their sadness and worry about the coming separation would probably stir up the same emotions in your mind.

When we die, we go alone—no one, not even our closest, dearest loved one, can accompany us. And being unable to accept this and let go of our attachment to our loved ones will cause our mind to be in turmoil and make it very difficult to have a peaceful death.

Recognize the attachment you have to your family and friends. Try to realize that having strong attachment to people can be a hindrance to having a peaceful state of mind at the time of death, so it is better to work on decreasing this attachment and learning to let go.

8. Your possessions and enjoyments cannot help

Your mind will probably also think of your possessions and property, which occupy a great deal of your time while you are alive, and are a source of much pleasure and satisfaction. But can any of these things bring you comfort and peace at the time of death? Your wealth may be able to provide you with a private room in the hospital and the best medical care, but that is all it can do for you. It cannot stop death from happening, and when you die, you cannot take any of it with you, not even one cent. Not only will your possessions be unable to help you at the time of death, but your mind may be caught up in worries about them—who will get what, and whether or not they will take proper care of "your" things. So that will make it difficult to have a peaceful, detached state of mind as you are dying.

Contemplate these points, and see if you can understand the importance of learning to be less dependent on and attached to material things.

9. *Your own body cannot help*

Your body has been your constant companion since birth. You know it more intimately than anything or anyone else. You have cared for it and protected it, worried about it, kept it comfortable and healthy, fed it and cleaned it, experienced all kinds of pleasure and pain with it. It has been your most treasured possession.

But now you are dying and that means you will be separated from it. It will become weak and eventually quite useless: your mind will separate from it and it will be taken to the cemetery or crematorium. What good can it possibly do you now?

Contemplate the strong sense of dependence and attachment you have to your body and how it cannot benefit you in any way at death. Regret about leaving it, and fear, will only compound your suffering.

By meditating on the final three points, we should come to realize how important it is to work on reducing our attachment to the things of this life, such as family and friends, possessions, and our body. We should also realize how important it is to take care of our mind, as that is the only thing that will continue to the next life. "Taking care of the mind" means working on decreasing the negative states of mind such as anger and attachment, and cultivating positive qualities such as faith, loving-kindness, compassion, patience, and wisdom.

Furthermore, as the imprints of our actions in this life will also go with our mind to the next one, and will determine the kind of rebirth and experiences we will have, it is essential to try our best to refrain from negative actions, and create positive actions as much as possible during our life.

It is possible that you will feel fear or sadness when doing this meditation. In one sense, that is good—it shows that you have taken the ideas seriously and have contemplated them well. Also, it is important to get in touch with how you *do* feel about death so that you can work on being prepared for it when it happens. By working on our mind, we can transcend fear, sadness, attachment, and other emotions that make it difficult to die with a peaceful mind.

Fear arises because of clinging to the idea of a permanent self—there is no such thing, so this is a delusion that just makes us suffer. If we keep death in mind in an easy, open way—accepting it as a natural and inevitable aspect of life—this clinging will gradually loosen, allowing us to be mindful and make every action positive and beneficial, for ourselves and others. And an awareness of death gives us enormous energy to not waste our life, but to live it as effectively as possible.

Dedication Conclude the meditation with the optimistic thought that you have every possibility to make your life meaningful and positive and thus will be able to die with peace of mind.

Remember the motivation you had at the beginning of the meditation and dedicate the merit of doing the meditation to that same purpose—for the benefit of all beings.

5
Meditation on Karma

Do not commit any nonvirtuous actions,
Perform only perfect virtuous actions,
Subdue your mind thoroughly—
This is the teaching of the Buddha.
—The Dhammapada

If everything is empty of inherent, independent existence, then why are we sometimes happy, and at other times depressed and miserable? Why do good things and bad things happen to people? One explanation is that ignorance of the empty nature of things still pervades our minds, and until we free our minds from ignorance we will continue to have problems. But another explanation is that, although everything is empty on the ultimate level of reality, on the relative or conventional level the experiences we have are subject to the law of cause and effect, or karma.

Karma is a Sanskrit word that means "action"—it refers to the process whereby the actions we do are the causes of effects or results that we will experience in the future. Positive actions lead to positive results such as good rebirths in our future lives, being healthy, getting what we need and want, and being treated well by others; negative actions lead to unfortunate results such as bad rebirths, health problems, failure to get what we need and want, and being abused by others.

The law of karma is also known as the law of cause and effect. But when we use the word "law" it should be understood as a natural law, like the law of gravity, rather than a law that was invented by anyone such as the Buddha. Through his meditative insights, Buddha became aware of the law of karma and explained it to us so that we could have more control over our lives and experiences. If we learn about karma and do our best to refrain from negative actions and do positive actions, then we will experience more happiness and less suffering. The results of our actions follow naturally, just as we enjoy good health from eating nutritious food, but get sick if we eat unhealthy or contaminated food. There is no one who rewards us for positive actions or punishes us for negative actions.

Some common questions and misconceptions about karma

People sometimes wonder if the law of karma applies only to those who believe in it, but not to those who do not know about or believe in it. If that were the case, it would be better not to know about karma, and the Buddha would have done us a disservice by talking about it! In reality, karma is a universal law that applies to all beings, whether they know about and believe in it or not. It is similar to gravity—all beings are subject to gravity, whether they are aware of it or not—or to poison—whoever eats poison will get sick, whether or not they believe that it's harmful.

Another common question is whether karma means that we have no free will. For those who are unaware of karma, there is little or no free will because they don't know the causes of good and bad experiences. Although they want happiness and success and don't want problems, they may avoid creating the causes of happiness—being honest and generous, for example—and may do the very things that bring problems—such as lying and cheating. On the other hand, those who know about karma are free to act in ways that will bring the happiness they wish for, and avoid the problems they don't want. So karma means that *we* are the creator: *we* are responsible for our experiences, rather than an external creator, or other people and circumstances.

Some people have the idea that since everything is empty, there is no good and bad, no right and wrong. This idea is totally mistaken, and also extremely detrimental to our spiritual development. Enlightened beings and those who have a direct, non-conceptual realization of emptiness see all things as having the same nature: emptiness of inherent existence. But emptiness does not negate the relative, conventional level of things. Things still exist on the relative level, and their existence is subject to the law of dependent arising: they exist in dependence on other things, such as causes and conditions. On the ultimate level, things are empty, but relatively, there is suffering and confusion, which is the result of negative actions, and there is happiness, which is the result of positive actions. So karma, cause and effect, definitely exists, and we would be wise to live according to it!

Some people have no trouble accepting karma; they may even have had an intuitive understanding of it their whole life. Others are sceptical and ask for proof. But it's difficult to come up with concrete proof because karma is in the mind, and the mind is non-material. The way it works is that when we do an action with our body, speech, or mind, a subtle imprint is left on our mind-stream, similar to the imprint left on camera-film when we take a picture. Later, when we encounter the right causes and conditions, that mental imprint will manifest in the form of experiences that occur in our mind, similar to the pictures that materialize when the film is developed.

Lama Yeshe said that we can see the workings of karma in our own life. When we're in a bad state of mind—dissatisfied with ourselves and our life, or angry at the world—then everything will go wrong and we will attract problems. But when we're in a good state of mind and treat people with respect and consideration, we're much more likely to have good experiences. So our own experiences are proof that our attitudes and behavior affect what happens to us in our daily life.

If you have difficulty accepting karma, it could be useful to check your reasons, and ask yourself if they are good, solid reasons. For example, you might find it difficult to accept because it's a foreign concept, one you didn't hear about from your family or education system. Is that a valid reason for rejecting something?

Some people find the idea of karma uncomfortable. They may think, "If I have lots of problems in my life, that means I must have done lots of bad things in the past, so I must be a bad person." This is an incorrect conclusion. There is no such thing as a "bad person." The minds of all unenlightened beings are afflicted with ignorance and other delusions that motivate us to act in unskillful ways, creating problems for ourselves and others, but this is not our true way of being. We all have the potential to become free of ignorance, delusions, and karma, and to become fully awakened, compassionate beings. We can't undo what was done in the past, but we can change ourselves from now on, and the teachings on karma show us how to start doing this.

People sometimes focus more on the negative side of karma—"you do bad things and bad things will happen to you." But we shouldn't forget the positive side of karma. It's important to remember all the good things about our life—the very fact that we have a human life, relatively good health, people who are kind and helpful to us, the opportunity to learn and practice spiritual teachings—and realize that these came about because we created lots of good karma in the past, and we can continue to create good karma in this life as well.

The purpose of meditating on karma is twofold: to develop the awareness that we are responsible—we are the creators of our own experiences—and to learn which actions bring suffering, so we can avoid those, and which actions lead to happiness, so that we can engage in those.

The practice

Sit comfortably and relax your body and mind. Let go of thoughts of the past and future, other places and people; resolve to keep your mind focused in the present, on your meditation.

Motivation Generate a positive motivation for doing the meditation, such as wanting to have a better understanding of karma so that you can avoid doing actions that bring problems to yourself and others, and can be more beneficial, both to yourself and others.

There are four aspects, or general principles, of karma. If you have time, meditate on all four in one session, or if time is short, take one every day over four days. As you reflect on each principle, bring to mind examples from your own life or stories you have heard to enrich your understanding. And do your best to reach a constructive conclusion, as explained at the end of every point.

1. Karma is definite

This means that there is a definite correlation between the actions we do and the experiences we have, in that negative actions bring problems, not happiness, and positive actions bring happiness, not suffering. It can never be otherwise. It is similar to what happens in nature: if we plant pumpkin seeds we get pumpkins, not chilli; and if we plant chilli seeds we get chillies, not pumpkins.

How do we know which actions are negative and which are positive? In the first two verses of the *Dhammapada (Collected Sayings)*, the Buddha explained that it depends on our state of mind, or motivation:

> Mind is the forerunner of all states;
> Mind is chief, mind-made are they.
> If one speaks or acts with an impure mind, suffering follows,
> Like the wheel that follows the cart-pulling ox.

> Mind is the forerunner of all states;
> Mind is chief, mind-made are they.
> If one speaks or acts with a pure mind, happiness follows,
> Like one's shadow that never leaves.

In other words, negative actions are those motivated by "impure minds" such as anger, attachment, jealousy and ignorance, and positive actions are those motivated by "pure minds" such as compassion, love, non-attachment and wisdom.

But the Buddha also explained ten actions that are by nature negative and lead to suffering: killing, stealing, sexual misconduct (which includes infidelity and abusive sexual behavior), lying, divisive speech, hurtful words, idle talk, covetousness, harmful intent and incorrect views (such as rejecting karma or the existence of enlightenment). There is a corresponding list of ten positive actions, which involve making the conscious effort to refrain from the ten negative ones with the recognition that they lead to suffering: that is, consciously refraining from killing, stealing, and so forth. Other examples of positive actions are helping those who are sick, poor, depressed, or grieving, being generous, ethical, and patient, and doing spiritual practices with a pure motivation.

Think back over your life and see if you can recall having done any of the ten negative actions, and try to recognize that although these actions may have brought you some short-term benefit, in the long-run they will bring problems. Bring to mind instances of positive actions you have done, and be glad about these, understanding that they are the cause of happiness, for yourself and others. Try to feel, "If I do negative actions such as killing or saying hurtful words to others, I plant seeds that will bring the bitter fruit of bad experiences and suffering, but if I do positive actions such as protecting life and being truthful, I plant seeds that will bring the sweet fruit of good experiences and happiness. Therefore I should try my best to avoid doing negative actions, and create as many positive actions as possible."

2. Karma increases

This means that if we do a negative action, even a minor one, and do not apply any opponent force such as purification practice, the karma increases continuously and will bring many unpleasant results. And on the positive side, one small positive action, if not opposed by a negative one, will bring many positive results. It is similar to what we can observe in nature: if we plant one tiny apple seed, eventually we will have a huge tree bearing many flowers and fruits every year, and if we let weeds grow unchecked in our garden, pretty soon they will take over.

The Buddha explained this principle in the *Dhammapada:*

> *Even a tiny evil deed*
> *Can cause great ruin and trouble*
> *In the world that lies beyond—*
> *Like poison that has entered the body.*

> *Even small meritorious acts*
> *Bring happiness to future lives,*
> *Accomplishing a great purpose*
> *Like seeds becoming bounteous crops.*

In general, there are four results of any action we do:

1. the fully ripened result
2. the result similar to the cause in terms of experience
3. the result similar to the cause in terms of action
4. the environmental result

To illustrate these, let's take the negative action of killing. The *fully ripened result* of killing is a rebirth in an unfortunate situation, with continuous problems and suffering. The *results similar to the cause in terms of experience* are unpleasant experiences that would occur in later, human lives, such as having a short life (for example, you might be killed or die of illness at a young age), many health problems, and constant failure. The *result similar to the cause in terms of action* is having the instinctive tendency to kill. This is actually the worst result, because it leads us to continue creating the same karma again and again, and thus we will experience the same results again and again. We can see this result even in our present life—the more we do a certain action, the easier it becomes to do it again, and soon it becomes habitual and even automatic. The *environmental result* of killing is being born or living in a violent, war-torn, or unhealthy environment.

Conversely, if we refrain from killing we will experience the opposite results: rebirth in good conditions, having good health and a long life, success in our activities and endeavors, living in peaceful, healthy environments, and having the natural tendency to cherish and protect the lives of others.

Contemplate these points and see if you can come to the conclusion that it is important to refrain from even small negative actions like telling "little white lies," and to not overlook opportunities to do even small positive actions, like giving ten cents to a homeless person or bread crumbs to some birds.

3. If we do not do an action, we will not experience its result

This means that if we don't do negative actions, we will not have bad experiences in the future. This principle explains why it is that some are killed or injured in a car accident while others walk away without a scratch; or why some fail in starting a business even though they have an MBA while others are successful even though they never set foot in a business school.

On the other hand, if we do not do any positive actions, we will not experience any good results in the future. Wishing to be happy and successful but not creating the right causes would be like wishing for flowers or vegetables to grow in our garden but not doing the work of planting the seeds, watering the small shoots, removing the weeds, and so on.

This principle can also be understood in terms of our present experiences. Any time we experience a problem or any unhappy state of mind, this is necessarily due to negative karma we created in the past. If we can understand and accept this, we will stop feeling like a victim and blaming others when problems happen to us. And all the good experiences in our life—being born human, enjoying good health, having enough food to eat, people being kind to us, and so forth—are the results of positive karma we created in the past. It's wise to feel joyful about this, and aspire to continue doing the same in this life.

By contemplating this point, realize that if you wish for happiness and good experiences in the future, you must do positive actions, and if you wish to avoid problems and unhappiness, you must avoid doing negative actions.

4. Karma is never lost

When we do an action—physical, verbal, or mental—an imprint, like a seed, is planted in our mind. Unless we do something to counteract that karmic seed, it will remain in the mind, even for many lifetimes, until we encounter the right causes and conditions for it to ripen in the form of experiences, good or bad. The Buddha said in the *Dhammapada*:

> *If you have done something wrong*
> *Or are involved in wrong*
> *And run away hoping to hide the fact,*
> *It is no use; there is no escape.*
> *There exists no place at all,*
> *But what you have done will follow you,*
> *In the oceans, through the skies,*
> *Or far off in mountain caves....*
>
> *Whether it was good or bad,*
> *The power of any action*
> *Once performed is never lost;*
> *The results arise accordingly.*

How can karmic seeds be counteracted? We can clear away negative karma by doing a purification practice using the four opponent powers (see pages 90 and 219): feeling regret, relying on helpful objects of refuge such as the Buddha, Dharma, and Sangha, doing positive actions to balance things out, and resolving to not do the action again. It is recommended that we do a purification practice every day, before going to sleep, to purify whatever negative actions we did during the day. But we can also purify negative karma created days, months, or years ago, in our childhood, or even in past lives—it's never too late!

Good karmic seeds can be lost by getting angry or generating incorrect views (such as rejecting karma or the possibility of attaining enlightenment), so it's wise to guard our mind from such attitudes. But since it is difficult to completely avoid them—especially anger—we can protect the positive karma we have created by dedicating it to a beneficial goal, especially to the enlightenment of all beings.

Conclude your contemplation of this principle by resolving to clear up past and present negative karma by doing purification practice, and to protect the good karma you create by dedicating it to the enlightenment of all beings.

When first contemplating karma, we may feel a sense of heaviness and even fear; similar to the way we would feel if our doctor told us we have a serious illness. But just as there are methods for dealing with illness—medicine, treatments, dietary and lifestyle changes, and working on our mind to learn to accept it—there are methods for working on karma. Remember, it is not like fate, fixed and unchangeable, so it can be changed. There is no negative karma that cannot be purified. Angulimala, who lived at the time of the Buddha, killed 999 people but was able to clear up that karma and attain nirvana, and the great Tibetan saint and poet Milarepa was responsible for the deaths of thirty-five people and many animals, but was able to purify that karma and attain enlightenment in that very lifetime. So whatever we have done in this or past lives can definitely be repaired and cleared out of the way of our spiritual progress.

Dedication End the session with this optimistic thought, and dedicate the positive energy of your meditation to all beings: may you and everyone else become free from suffering and its causes, karma and delusions, and attain enlightenment as soon as possible.

6
Purifying Negative Karma

After meditating on karma (previous chapter) we'll probably feel uncomfortable about the negative actions we have done and the consequences we are likely to face in the future. But there is a solution to this—the practice of purification. Negative karma is not something fixed, permanent, and irreparable. The imprints left on our mind from our negative actions can be purified so that we don't have to experience the suffering results that would otherwise come, and so we can clear this negative energy out of the way of our spiritual development. That is the reason for the practice of purification.

There is no negativity that cannot be purified. The purification process is basically a psychological one. As Lama Yeshe says, it is our mind (and on the basis of that, our actions) that creates the negativity, and it is our mind that transforms it by creating positive energy. Although in Buddhism we rely on Buddha's methods for purification, it is not the Buddha who purifies us; we ourselves, as Lama says, do the work. We created the karma, and only we can clean it up.

The practice of purification involves contemplating the four opponent powers: regret, reliance, remedy, and resolve. It is best to do a practice of purification every day—for example, at the end of the day—to clear up whatever negative karma we created that day, as well as negativities from the past.

1. The power of regret

Regret involves recognizing that certain actions we have done are negative because they harmed others and/or ourselves, because they will bring more problems later on, and also because we were acting in an ego-centered, deluded way. Regret is not the same as guilt. Guilt comes from not understanding the true nature of things, and believing that we have a real, permanent self or "I." We focus on things we have done wrong, or things we feel we should have done but didn't do, and we feel "I'm bad, and I will always be this way." Guilt may also cause us to feel that we don't deserve to be happy. It tends to be emotional rather than rational and intelligent. It's not helpful to feel guilty—it doesn't bring any positive results, but only makes us miserable and blocks our spiritual development.

Regret on the other hand is intelligent and constructive. It is based on the understanding of karma: that negative actions such as killing or hurting others cause suffering to them as well as to ourselves, both now and in the future. Harming others disturbs our mind—we're going against our true, pure nature—and leaves imprints that will ripen as more problems and suffering in the future. Whatever problems and unwanted experiences we've had in this life are the results of negative actions we did in the past, and the negative actions we do now are the cause of future suffering. Who wants that? So logically, what we need to do is feel regret and clean up our karma!

Regret is likened to the way we would feel if we found out that something we had swallowed was poisonous. Fearful of getting sick or losing our life, we would drop everything and rush to our doctor or the emergency room to rid ourselves of the poison. In the same way, negative karma is highly toxic: it poisons our mind and our spiritual development, and brings unwanted troubles in the future. Understanding this, we regret our mistakes and do whatever we can to clear up the karma.

2. The power of reliance

When we fall down on the ground, we rely on the ground to get up again. Similarly, when we do something negative, it's either in relation to pure beings such as the Buddha or our spiritual teacher (Sanskrit: guru), or in relation to ordinary sentient beings, so in order to purify our negative karma, we need to recall and rely upon those two objects. First, we rely on the Buddha, who is like the doctor whose medicine we take to purify our deluded actions. It's not that we need Buddha to forgive us (although he always does anyway); rather, we rely on him by taking refuge in him (see page 168) and using the methods he taught to purify ourselves and to change our life and our behavior to a more positive direction.

For someone who's not a Buddhist, this first step could involve renewing your commitment to follow the guidance of whoever is your object of devotion, or re-dedicating yourself to whatever positive goals you aspire to live by. It is also very effective to confess your misdoings to someone you trust, such as a spiritual teacher.

Second, we rely on other beings—the very beings we have harmed, in this life and in the past—by developing compassion and love for them. You can think about how they are basically just like you: they don't want to experience the slightest suffering or problem, and they only want to be happy and peaceful. Then, generate the sincere determination to try your best to avoid harming others, and instead do what you can to help them.

3. The power of remedy

This means doing something positive in order to counteract the negative energy we have created. In general, any positive action can be used to purify our negative karma, but certain practices are particularly powerful remedies. These include visualizing figures such as Shakyamuni Buddha (page 186), Vajrasattva (page 219), or the Thirty-five Buddhas (page 238) and reciting their names and / or mantras. The meditations on love (page 111), compassion (page 116), and emptiness (page 53) can also be used—the latter is actually said to be the best antidote to negativity, although it is difficult and may not be suitable for beginners. A simpler method is the purification meditation using the breath on page 37. Choose one of these methods every time you do a session of purification practice.

You can also do more engaged activities such as volunteer work or making donations to charitable causes. Saving lives—for example, rescuing animals or insects who are in danger of dying or being killed, or caring for the ill—is particularly effective to counteract the karma of killing. It is also good to apologize and make amends to the people you have harmed, if this is possible.

4. The power of resolve

The fourth step is an extremely important one: making the determination not to repeat the same negative actions again. Without this, it's very hard to change, to give up our old bad habits. Determination to not harm again is like a beacon that guides our body, speech, and mind in new directions. As Lama Zopa Rinpoche says, "We can mold our minds into any shape we like."

With the heavier negative actions, such as killing and stealing, you may be able to resolve never to do them again for the rest of your life. (Of course, this means resolving to give up doing such actions *intentionally*. It's impossible to avoid certain unintentional actions, such as killing insects we can't see while we are walking or driving.)

However, with those actions that are more habitual and hard to stop, such as lying or losing your temper, you need to be realistic. It's better to resolve to not do them for shorter periods of time, like five minutes or an hour. You can then gradually increase the length of time of such promises—a half-day, then one day, and so on.

Then resolve in general to make the effort to avoid the old habits. This determination not to do negative actions again is what gives us the strength to turn ourselves around. We need to have confidence in our ability to change, one step at a time.

The practice

Sit comfortably and relax. Spend some time focusing on the breath to calm your mind and center it in the present.

Motivation Then generate a positive motivation for doing the practice, such as "I am doing this meditation not just for myself, but for others—to learn to be less harmful, and more helpful, to them."

Take as much time as you need to contemplate each of the four powers thoroughly, to generate the right state of mind for each point.

1. The power of regret

Think back over the day, from the time you woke up this morning, and try to remember anything you did that was negative. Start with actions of the body, such as killing or causing physical suffering to any being; taking something that did not belong to you, or not paying money you owed, like a bus fare; or engaging in inappropriate sexual behavior.

Then check if you did anything negative with your speech, such as lying, exaggerating, or being deceitful, saying words that caused bad feelings between people, saying things that were hurtful or upsetting to someone, or spending time gossiping or talking about insignificant things.

Then see if you can remember negative thoughts you may have indulged in, such as wishing harm on somebody or feeling happy at their misfortune; having critical, judgmental thoughts toward anyone, including yourself; feeling dissatisfied with what you have and wishing for more or better, or for what someone else has; in short, any states of mind that involved hatred, anger, greed, jealousy, arrogance, selfishness, and so forth.

Also bring to mind any negative actions you recall doing in past days, months, and years, going as far back in your life as you can. Generate sincere regret, from the depths of your heart, for all these actions, by understanding that they are the cause of suffering—in some cases to others, and in all cases to yourself. These actions planted imprints on your mind that will ripen as problems and misfortune in the future. They also impede your progress on the spiritual path, and prolong your existence in an imperfect, unsatisfactory situation. Realize that no one wants to suffer, and these are the very things that bring suffering, so acknowledge your mistakes and feel a sincere wish to rectify them.

2. The power of reliance

If there is a holy being or higher power endowed with unconditional love, compassion, and wisdom toward whom you feel respect and confidence, then bring them to mind. Acknowledge your mistakes and the difficulty you have refraining from negative actions and attitudes on your own. Ask for help and guidance so that you can change yourself and give up these negativities from now on.

Alternatively, you can bring to mind the ethical principles that you believe in but acted against, and renew your commitment to follow them.

Then, for the negative actions you did to others, generate love and compassion. Contemplate the fact that, just like you, others do not want to suffer and they wish to experience only happiness and peace. Feel how desirable it would be to stop harming them and instead be kind and helpful to them. Generate the altruistic wish to purify your negative actions and your delusions such as anger, greed, and selfishness, so that from now on you can only benefit others, not harm them.

3. The power of remedy

Now you need to do something positive to counteract the negative energy you created.

If you feel comfortable about visualizing an enlightened being, as mentioned above, you can visualize a figure such as Buddha or Vajrasattva above your head. While reciting the appropriate mantra, imagine light flowing down from the figure, filling your entire body and mind and purifying all your negative karma and delusions.

If you do not feel comfortable visualizing such a figure, you can imagine a sphere of light above your head, thinking that it represents all enlightened qualities and energies, and visualize light flowing down from it and filling you (as above). If you wish, you could recite the short mantra of Vajrasattva (om vajrasattva hum) or the mantra of Avalokiteshvara (om mani padme hum) while visualizing the light filling and purifying you.

Alternatively, you can do one of the other meditations suggested above, such as that on love; or decide to act in more positive ways in your daily life, such as being more helpful or generous.

4. The power of resolve

If you feel confident that you can completely give up some nega-tive actions, such as killing and stealing, make the promise to do that. But for those negative actions you cannot completely give up, either promise to give them up for a realistic period of time, or promise that you will do your very best to be mindful and avoid doing them.

Resolve to change your old emotional habits such as anger, jealousy, depression, criticalness, and attachment. Feel confident in your ability to change, but at the same time understand that it takes time to change, so don't have unrealistic expectations.

Dedication At the end of the meditation session dedicate all the positive energy you have created by doing this purification practice to all living beings, that they may become free from all their suffering and its causes: negative karma and delusions.

(There are two other purification practices later in the book: a meditation on the Buddha Vajrasattva, also practiced in the context of the four powers, on page 219; and a simpler meditation on page 147.)

7

Meditation on Suffering

The question of suffering has always perplexed philosophers and theologians—not to mention ordinary suffering human beings like us! Why is there so much fighting in the world? Why so much starvation, sickness, inequality, and injustice? What are the causes of suffering? The Buddhist view can be summarized as what are known as the four noble truths.

First, *suffering exists.* Every sentient being suffers to some degree or other. "Suffering" does not refer merely to severe pain or problems; it refers to any experience that is unpleasant or unsatisfactory.

Second, *suffering always has a cause.* The principal causes of suffering are karma (previous actions of our body, speech, or mind) and delusions (disturbing states of mind such as anger, attachment, and ignorance).

Third, *there is an end to suffering.* We all have the potential to reach a state of perfect peace, clarity, and compassion, in which we no longer experience the results of past negative acts or create the causes for future suffering.

Fourth, *there is a means to end suffering.* The way to end suffering is to gradually abandon its causes—anger, selfishness, attachment, and other negative states of mind, and actions motivated by these—and cultivate the causes of happiness—patience, love, non-attachment, generosity, and the other positive states of mind. And finally, by developing insight into the true nature of all things, we can eliminate the very root of suffering: the ignorance that sees everything in a mistaken way.

"Suffering" refers to all degrees of unsatisfactory physical and psychological experiences. There are many ways to meditate on suffering and all are for the purpose of generating a deep sense of its extensiveness; how, in varying degrees, it permeates our own lives and the lives of all others.

The purpose of developing this awareness is not to increase our misery. On the contrary, successful meditation on suffering brings us to a more realistic view of life. And by understanding that the causes of suffering lie in our own attitudes and actions, we will gradually come to see that unraveling the complexities of our mind and thus developing control over our thoughts and actions is both desirable and possible.

Our usual view of life is unrealistic. Most of our pleasant experiences depend on external objects and situations, whose very nature is ephemeral. When these things change or disappear we cling on, unwilling to accept the reality of the situation. We want pleasure to last and are disappointed when it doesn't. And so we go, up and down, from pleasure to pain, happiness to unhappiness, all our lives.

Awareness of this reality is a step toward eliminating suffering. We will stop expecting people and things to make us happy and instead see that it is our attitude toward them that determines happiness and satisfaction. Ironically, when we stop clinging unrealistically to things, we enjoy them all the more!

Another major benefit of this meditation is that we can see that others suffer in the same way, and as a result we inevitably develop more kindness and compassion toward them.

But the main purpose of recognizing the suffering of our lives is to develop the strong intention to do what is necessary to be finally free of it. All unhappy, painful experiences are rooted in the ignorance that believes everything exists inherently, in and of itself. Seeing the emptiness, the lack, of this way of existing cuts through all confusion and problems.

Gaining this understanding, however, is no simple matter. It requires tremendous energy to concentrate the mind on the nature of things, to cut through our habitual perception of them to reach their ultimate, pure reality. The fuel that drives us in this task is the desire to free ourselves, and others, from all suffering.

The practice

Motivation Sit comfortably and relax. Generate a positive motivation for doing the meditation, such as wishing to better understand suffering in order to do what is necessary to free everyone—yourself and others—from all problems, pain, and unhappiness.

There are three aspects of suffering to contemplate. Go through each one as slowly as you like. Don't just make a mental checklist of the points but bring your emotions and intuition into the meditation; really feel every example of suffering as if you were experiencing it right now.

1. The suffering of suffering

This includes all obvious forms of suffering, physical and mental, such as the severe sufferings arising from war, terrorism, natural disasters, famine, violent crime, rape, abuse, imprisonment, poverty, injustice, racism, addiction, injury, and illness.

But it also includes all the normal, everyday problems your body experiences: aches and pains, heat and cold, hunger and thirst, bad eyesight, earaches, cuts and burns, weight problems, muscle tension, fatigue—the list is endless. Recall these experiences and how we are rarely without one or more of them.

There may be more extreme kinds of physical suffering that you experienced in the past—bring these to mind and see the possibility that they could happen again; there is no guarantee they will not.

Think of the physical suffering you will experience when you are old. Picture yourself at the age of eighty or ninety, your body degenerated and wrinkled and not functioning properly. Finally, there is death. Think of the different ways you could die and the suffering of the body then.

Contemplate the fact that it is the nature of the body to change, meet with pain, degenerate, and eventually die. Therefore it is unrealistic and unwise to be attached to it, and to cling to it as "me."

Now look at mental and emotional suffering. Bring to mind past or present experiences of loneliness, depression, grief, frustration, jealousy, anger, fear, confusion, anxiety. Go back over your life and see that rarely was there a time when you were not experiencing at least some of these emotions.

Now look at your state of mind at this moment. Are you anxious? Depressed? Angry? Confused? Agitated? Think of the mental suffering that is likely to come in the future when people close to you die or leave you, when you yourself die, or when the myriad other things occur in our lives that are likely to cause unhappiness to one degree or another.

Expand your thoughts to include the experiences of others. At this very moment all beings in existence, simply because they have a confused mind and a perishable body, are going through some form of mental or physical pain—from the slightest discomfort to the grossest suffering.

Start with the people you know—your friends, relatives and neighbors. Some are sick, some old; others are depressed, anxious, dissatisfied, lonely. Then think about the people you don't know, whose lives are plagued by war, poverty, unemployment, racism, disease, political oppression.

We also share this world with animals and other creatures. Contemplate their day-to-day suffering: hunger, pain, cold, lack of freedom, fear of being killed.

Become aware that all of these countless living beings have a stream of consciousness not so different from your own: we all react with joy to kindness and beauty, with fear to pain and harm, and with anger to whatever threatens the peace of ourselves and our loved ones. We all try to be happy and to avoid problems, but as long as we are unenlightened we meet with one suffering situation after another.

2. The suffering of change

This more subtle level of suffering refers to the experiences we normally think of as pleasure or happiness. They are called "suffering" because they do not last. Every nice experience comes to an end without fully satisfying us or relieving our problems. It leads, instead, to the desire to repeat it, in the hope that we will find the satisfaction we are looking for.

Think of any pleasant experience: a nice meal, sex, a day at the beach, skiing, music, a movie, a cigarette, a beautiful sunset—how long does the pleasure last? Are any of these experiences fully satisfying? If you think they *are* fully satisfying, then why do you repeat them again and again?

Another reason pleasant experiences are considered "suffering" is because they are not true, pure pleasure. If they were, the pleasure would continue, and even increase, the more we engaged in them. Is this what happens, or does the pleasure decrease and even turn into misery? For example, when you are hungry and eat something, at first you feel good because the discomfort of hunger diminishes, but what would happen if you kept eating more and more? You would feel increasingly uncomfortable, and may even become sick! And even if you eat just the right amount to be comfortably full, that experience doesn't last: a few hours later the hunger comes back and you need to eat again.

When we get together with friends or family, at first we are happy, talking and laughing, enjoying each other's company. But what would happen if we continued to stay together, hour after hour, day after day, without a break? We would probably become bored, irritated, and might even start arguing. Even sitting comfortably in a chair: eventually we need to change position because the comfort turns to discomfort. Or sitting by a fire on a chilly day: at first it is such a pleasure, but soon we must move away because it becomes too hot.

Look carefully at your life to see whether or not this is true. Recall some good experiences: did they last? Did they truly satisfy you? If the pleasure is true pleasure, why doesn't it stay with you indefinitely? Can you think of any example of unchangeable, lasting happiness in your life or in anyone else's?

Contemplate how everything changes; how pleasurable experiences do not last but lead inevitably to dissatisfaction, irritation, boredom, or loneliness. From one point of view, compared to the suffering of suffering, these experiences are pleasant. But from

another point of view, compared to the pure, lasting bliss of liberation and enlightenment, these experiences are another kind of
suffering.

It is the very nature of all things that they change and eventually
come to an end. Even a blissful relationship has its ups and downs
and will end with separation or death. Beautiful people grow old
and grey and eventually die. Power does not last and wealth runs
out. Flowers wither, sunsets fade, parties end.

Conclude this part of the meditation by firmly deciding that it
is not reasonable to cling to any person or object as a means of
finding lasting satisfaction, and that clinging, instead, brings the
very opposite result.

3. All-pervading suffering

This is even more subtle than the suffering of change. It refers to
our very existence as ordinary, unenlightened beings, with our
mind caught up inextricably in delusions and karma. Although the
nature of our mind is clear and has the potential to experience the
pure, enduring peace and bliss of enlightenment, we are unable
to keep it free of disturbed, unhappy thoughts and feelings even
for an hour, or a few minutes. And although we want nothing but
pleasant, happy experiences, it's impossible to go through life, or
even one day, without experiencing problems. Why is this?

Lacking a direct, intuitive insight into the true nature of things,
we think, speak, and act under the control of delusions, our habitual negative tendencies. We are thus in a bind: on the one hand,
we experience in every moment the effects of previous karma and
delusions and, on the other, we create every moment the causes
for future effects. This very moment of existence is both the effect
of past suffering and the cause of suffering in the future.

The situation of being stuck in this cycle, this complex web of
problems, is itself all-pervading suffering. It can be compared
to being in a prison, locked in by our karma and delusions. In
prison there can be terrible experiences like being attacked by

other prisoners or sadistic guards—these are like the sufferings of suffering. Sometimes there are pleasant experiences, such as watching a good movie, or getting a visit from a loved one—these are like the suffering of change. But no matter what one experiences, pleasant or unpleasant, one is stuck in prison and not free to go where one wants or do as one likes, and this is like all-pervading suffering.

Let your mind absorb this idea. Generate a strong feeling for the self-perpetuating dilemma that is your existence.

Then contemplate how there are countless living beings caught up in this seemingly endless cycle, just as you are.

But don't panic. The situation is not hopeless! There is a way out of this cycle. Just as there is a cause of suffering—our false view of the way things exist—there is necessarily a cause of the *end* of this suffering, an antidote. The final antidote is to develop the right understanding of the nature of reality and thus cut through our confusion and our habit of following the ego's whims.

In the meantime, we can use our life and energy in positive ways: helping others with love and generosity, and increasing the positive thoughts and attitudes in our mind. And by refraining from negative actions and counteracting harmful attitudes in our mind as they arise, we avoid creating further causes of suffering. As our understanding of reality grows, so too does our detachment from ordinary, transient things, and our web of confusion gradually untangles. Finally, this understanding becomes a direct, intuitive perception of emptiness, which eliminates, once and for all, the very root of suffering.

Draw conclusions from any insights you may have had during this meditation. Acknowledging the painful, dissatisfactory nature of life is quite difficult, but it is the only way out. Until we stop running away from the reality of suffering and learn to deal honestly with the rough, unsubdued aspects of our mind, we will continue to circle in confusion. Awareness of suffering gives us the energy we need to penetrate the nature of reality.

Thus, conclude your session optimistically, with the determination to use your life skillfully and do what you can to overcome suffering.

Dedication Dedicate all your good intentions and energy to the growth of insight in yourself and all others.

Practical application

We have plenty of opportunities in our day-to-day lives to familiarize ourselves with the ideas presented in this meditation. Every day we experience a multitude of troubles: hunger, tiredness, aches and pains, irritation, boredom, frustration. Our usual reaction is to get rid of or by-pass these problems as quickly as possible. But it is a good idea—before reaching for a painkiller, turning on the TV, checking what's in the fridge, or seeking out a friend—to spend a few minutes just *experiencing* the pain: "So, this is suffering!"

Because we habitually avoid confronting and dealing with pain, it is difficult in meditation to take a good, honest look at the reality of suffering. Therefore, we should learn to use our actual experiences, as they occur, to deepen our understanding of the subject.

This does not mean that we should regard life as one big tragedy or go around always miserable and tense. We can be aware of suffering and still keep a sense of humor. Happiness and suffering are both impermanent, transitory experiences. We should not emphasize one over the other, but acknowledge the changeable nature of both.

So, when we find ourselves grasping unrealistically at a new person in our life, say, we should remind ourselves that the happiness we're experiencing is transitory and cannot eliminate all our problems, anyway. With this attitude, which is more realistic and less exaggerated, we will probably enjoy the experience all the more!

When there is a problem, physical or psychological, we can think, "It's transitory—at some point it will be gone. But problems and suffering will continue to happen to me until I work on my mind and eliminate all causes of suffering. This problem reminds me of the need to look after my actions—refraining from negative karma and creating positive karma as much as I can." By doing this, the problem becomes a teaching.

When people around us are suffering, we should be sensitive and compassionate and help them to the best of our ability. But we should not get so involved that their problem becomes our problem and we grow tense and worried over it. We can avoid this by recalling that the cause, and the solution, of any problem lie in the mind of the person experiencing it. It's up to them to work their way out of it. As long as we are loving and kind and do whatever we can to ease their pain, we should not feel guilty or inadequate and think we must do more.

In short, suffering and problems are not necessarily bad; it depends on our attitude. If we feel averse to them and see them as completely useless and unwanted, then we'll suffer more. But if we have a more realistic view, seeing them as a natural part of life, then we can accept them calmly. In addition, by learning to use them in our path of spiritual growth, we can even feel glad when they occur.

8

Equanimity Meditation

The goal of Mahayana practice is to reach the state of perfect wholeness, enlightenment, in order to alleviate the suffering of others, bring them happiness, and finally lead them to their own enlightenment. The aspiration to do this is known as "the mind of enlightenment" (Sanskrit: *bodhichitta*), and is the experience of opening our heart to all beings, allowing love and compassion to flow to everyone, without limitation. A person who possesses bodhichitta actually feels responsible for easing the suffering of all living beings and leading them to happiness.

We can start to cultivate the mind of enlightenment now, in our day-to-day lives, by being kind and open to the people we meet: being patient with them and aware of their needs. It is easy, however, to deceive ourselves, to play the role of a friendly, open person while hiding our feelings of irritation and intolerance. So it is important to get in touch with our feelings while also making an effort to extend ourselves to others, and this is done most effectivey in the concentration of meditation.

Normally, we discriminate: we either like, dislike, or are indifferent to everyone we meet. These reactions are mostly self-centered, based on whether the person appears agreeable, disagreeable, or uninteresting to *me*.

At the root of this discrimination is our instinctive misunderstanding of the way things exist, especially our own self. This problem has always been with us and we build on it elaborately throughout life, thinking, and believing, "I am this way and will always be; this is good for me and that brings me down."

Our belief in this I gives rise to the desire to protect and nourish it. Everything we do is for the sake of this self. It has needs that must be fulfilled; it must find happiness and avoid pain. The I likes this person because she makes it happy and dislikes that person because he causes it pain. Everything is seen from the perspective of this I's needs.

Our basic misapprehension of the I makes our perception faulty. If we analyze and search for the permanent, fixed self that seems to be there, we cannot find it; it is an illusion. There is only a fluctuating stream of mind and body traveling through life, experiencing joy, problems, love, frustration. We meet people, interact with them briefly in positive or negative ways, and then separate. Nothing lasts, nothing is stable.

The more we cling to this unreal I and try to fulfill its demands, the deeper we bury ourselves in problems and confusion. Our classification of people into "friends," "enemies," and "strangers" is probably the best example of this.

We assume that the person we like has inherently good qualities and the person we dislike is inherently bad. We behave as though these qualities are permanent and unchanging; as though we will always be close to the person we have labeled "friend" and never close to the person we dislike. And it is hard to imagine that an uninteresting person in the street could ever become a friend.

But these assumptions are mistaken, as our own experiences tell us. Relationships can and do change. People we were once close to are now impossible to communicate with, and others whom we couldn't bear the sight of are now dear friends.

People change, our thoughts and feelings change, situations change. The changes that make us see a friend as an enemy can occur from one minute to the next, one year to the next, one lifetime to the next. The reasons for seeing someone as friend, enemy, or stranger are not solid and incontrovertible. But holding onto them as if they were prevents us from seeing things as they really are and makes it difficult for us to deal with change when it occurs.

The following meditation has us examine our attitudes and feelings toward others in order to recognize where they are mistaken.
This can lead us gradually to a state of equanimity, in which our
mind is more balanced and less under the control of attachment to
loved ones, aversion and hatred toward enemies, and indifference
toward strangers.

The practice

Motivation Sit comfortably and generate the strong intention to
do this meditation in order to develop perfect equanimity for the
benefit of yourself and others. Perhaps you would like to say some
of the prayers on page 171–74.

Imagine in the space in front of you three people: someone you
like, someone you dislike, and someone you feel indifferent to.
Retain the images of the friend, enemy, and stranger throughout
the meditation.

First, focus on your friend, and ask yourself why you like this
person. See if you can recognize that your reasons are mainly
because of what she or he does for *you*.... Are those good reasons
for liking someone and holding them dear?

Then look at the person you dislike and examine your reasons
for feeling that way. Again, check if your ego is involved—for
example, the person may have harmed *you*, or may behave in ways
that *you* find unacceptable. Are those good reasons for disliking
someone, and treating them badly or wishing them harm?

Then look at the person you feel indifferent to—why do you
feel this way? Is your ego involved here as well? Is it because this
person has neither helped nor harmed *you*?

Also, ask yourself if you regard these relationships as permanent:
do you believe that you will always get along with your friend,
that you will never get along with your enemy, and that you will
always be distant from the stranger? Recall relationships you
had in the past that changed: a friend becoming an enemy or a
stranger, or vice versa.

Now imagine the friend visualized in front of you doing something hurtful or unacceptable…. Would your feelings toward this person change?

Recall that this person was not your friend before you became acquainted, and could very easily cease to be your friend in the future.

Realize that there is no sound reason for feeling kind and loving toward only the friend of this moment. Relationships changed in the past and will continue to change. Today's friend can become tomorrow's enemy.

Now turn your attention to your enemy, and imagine this person doing something kind or helpful, such as praising you for something you did, or helping you fix your car which has broken down…. Look carefully at your feelings for this person: are they softening? You *can* learn to feel warmly toward your enemy. This has happened before and will happen again. Why hold so strongly to the conception that this person is definitely "enemy?"

And what of the stranger? This relationship could go either way, but since we are trying to develop more positive feelings for others, imagine the stranger doing something helpful, such as giving you the right directions when you are lost, or returning your wallet which you dropped absent-mindedly…. How would this affect your feelings toward this person?

If you are able to accept the existence of past and future lifetimes, consider the idea that you have known these three people before, in other lifetimes, but in very different relationships. Consider that the friend of this lifetime may have been your enemy in another lifetime…. Your present enemy may have been someone very dear to you, a parent or sibling, or a close friend…. And the present stranger may have been both friend and enemy…. See how this affects your feelings toward these three people.

Understand that relationships are not permanent, but a loved one can become an enemy and vice versa, and a stranger can become either a friend or an enemy.

Also, no one is a friend, enemy, or stranger from their own side, independently; rather, they become so in dependence on how our mind labels them. Someone you regard as a friend is seen by others as an enemy, and there are people who love the person you regard as an enemy. Therefore, it is unwise to cling to these three types of people as if they were permanent and independently-existing.

It is also very helpful to recognize that in some ways, everyone is equal, exactly the same. One of these ways is that everyone wants to be happy and does not want any problems or pain. Contemplate this: your friend, enemy, and stranger all want happiness as much as you do, and, just like you, they do not want to experience even the smallest problem. And everyone, yourself and others, *deserves* to be happy and peaceful, and free from all suffering. Try to really feel this....

Another way in which all beings are equal is that we all have the potential to free our minds from all negativities, develop ourselves to the fullest, and achieve ultimate clarity and compassion. Everyone can, and *will*, become enlightened one day. Recognize that the differences we see in people are superficial, based on our mistaken and narrow self-centered viewpoint. If our thoughts and feelings were more in line with reality, we would see that everyone equally deserves our care and compassion.

None of this means that we should not discriminate; on a practical level it is necessary. Naturally we feel closer to some people and are wise to keep our distance from others. This is not a contradiction. The point of the meditation is to develop equal concern, equal regard, for everyone, whether they help or harm us at this point in time; and to see that our present discrimination is based on arbitrary, mistaken, and very changeable labels.

Dedication Finally, dedicate your positive energy and insight to the well-being and happiness of all.

9
Meditation on Love

Love, also called "loving-kindness," is wanting others to be happy. It is a natural quality of mind, but until we develop it through meditation and other practices it remains limited, reserved for a few select individuals—usually those we are attached to. Genuine love is universal in scope, extending to everyone, without exception.

Although we might agree with this idea in principle, we probably find it difficult to actualize. Does love arise spontaneously for all the people in the street and the supermarket? Do we feel love for the politicians we don't like, racists, parents who abuse their children, the people who harm us, who make our lives difficult? If not, we have work to do!

We should begin with mindfulness: observing our reactions to the people we encounter, looking out for feelings of attraction, aversion, and indifference. As long as we continue to discriminate between those we like, those we dislike, and those we do not care about we can never even take the first step.

To counteract this mistaken discrimination, we can practice the equanimity meditation (page 106) and the methods for dealing with attachment and anger (pages 124–34). The following meditation is a good complement to these; it helps us tap our natural resource of love and channel it to all living beings. If we practice it with concentration and sincerity, really getting in touch with our heart, we will find that it is possible to truly want others to be happy, regardless of their relationship to us.

The meditation has us start by visualizing our parents and other relatives beside us, and all other beings around us. This is a traditional Tibetan method for enhancing our bodhichitta motivation—it assumes that practitioners are on good terms with the people in their family. This is not true for everyone, however, so thinking of your mother, father, or other family members may give rise to anger or anxiety rather than love and compassion. If this is the case, it's not necessary to force yourself to visualize those individuals—you can either leave them out for now, or place them in front of you among your "enemies."

However, it *is* important to eventually resolve any problems we have with others, especially our immediate family, in order to fully progress on the path of spiritual development. So when you feel sufficient courage and strength to start working on those problems, you can do so using such meditations as equanimity, compassion, and dealing with negative energy. But be patient—it can sometimes take years of practice to resolve such problems, and if the emotions involved are very deep and painful, you may also need professional help.

Some meditations, such as those on the breath and emptiness, involve meditating *on* an object. Other meditations, such as those on love and compassion, involve transforming the mind *into* the object we're meditating on. So ideally when we do this meditation our mind truly experiences love. However, this is something that normally takes time and practice, so don't be frustrated if you don't feel anything initially. It's enough to simply think the thoughts and say the words "May you be happy, etc." By making your mind familiar with these, in time the feeling of love will arise naturally.

The practice

Sit comfortably. Relax your body and mind and let all thoughts and worries subside. Mindfully observe your breath until you are calm and your awareness is focused in the here-and-now.

Motivation Think that you are doing this meditation for the benefit of yourself and others: to generate more positive, loving energy
in your mind and to send it out to others, to the world.

Start by imagining all living beings around you: your mother is on
your left, your father on your right, and other relatives and friends
are around and behind you. Visualize in front of you those you
dislike or who have hurt you. And extending in every direction,
right to the horizon, are all other beings. Feel that they are there,
all in human form, sitting quietly, like you. If it is difficult to visualize *all* beings, think of as many as you can, comfortably. Stay
relaxed—don't feel crowded or tense, but imagine that a sense of
harmony and peace pervades everyone.

Consider how nice it would be, for yourself and others, if you
were able to love all these beings. Contemplate that everyone
wants to be happy and to avoid suffering, just as you do. They are
all trying to make the best of their lives, even those who are angry
and violent.

Now generate a feeling of love in your heart. You can do this
by thinking of someone you love and letting your natural good
feelings for this person arise. You might like to imagine your love
as a warm, bright light; not physical, but pure, positive energy
glowing in your heart.

Before you can truly love others you need to love yourself. Loving
yourself means accepting yourself as you are, with your present
faults and shortcomings, and recognizing you have the potential to
free yourself from all your problems. So, really wish yourself all the
happiness and goodness there is. Imagine that the warm energy in
your heart expands until it completely fills your body and mind.

If you have a habit of being critical, judgmental, and even angry
toward yourself, it will take time to change this, so you probably will
not suddenly feel love for yourself. But if you say to yourself "May I be
happy; may I have what I need to feel happy, safe, loved, and satisfied,"
and so forth, then gradually these thoughts and feelings will grow and
become genuine. It's enough for now to just think this way and say these
words to yourself…

Now meditate on love for others. Start with your family and close friends sitting near you. Say in your mind words such as: "May you be happy. May you have what you need to feel happy, safe, loved, and satisfied. May all your thoughts be positive and all your experiences good. May you be free of problems, sickness, and sadness. May your lives be long and peaceful and may you quickly reach enlightenment." Imagine the warm, luminous energy radiating from your body, touching them and filling their bodies and minds, bringing them the happiness they wish for. Again, don't worry if you don't actually feel love; it's enough to say these words and think these thoughts. In time the feeling will come.

Think next of some people you are not so close to. They could be people you work with, neighbors, fellow shoppers in the supermarket, fellow drivers on the road. Reflect that they, just like you, want to be happy, and deserve to be happy. See if you can feel the wish for them to be happy by thinking, "May you be happy. May you have what you need to feel happy, safe, loved, and satisfied. May all your thoughts be positive and all your experiences good. May you be free of problems, sickness, and sadness. May your lives be long and peaceful and may you quickly reach enlightenment." Then send the radiant energy of love from your heart to them and imagine that they experience the happiness they wish for.

Lastly, turn your attention to the people in front of you, those you have difficulty with. Contemplate that they also need and deserve your love. Wish them to be free of the confusion, anger, and self-centeredness that drive them to act the way they do. Really want them to find peace of mind, happiness, and finally enlightenment. Think, and try to feel sincerely, "May you be happy. May you have what you need to feel happy, safe, loved, and satisfied. May all your thoughts be positive and all your experiences good. May you be free of problems, sickness, and sadness. May your lives be long and peaceful and may you quickly reach enlightenment." Imagine that the radiant energy of love flows from your heart to them and that they experience the happiness they wish for.

Continue to send your positive, warm feelings out to all the other people around you. Love is an unlimited spring of good energy, so you shouldn't worry that it will run out! Completely open your heart and imagine your love flowing to every direction, reaching all the beings who are lonely, sick, hungry, confused, oppressed, frustrated, frightened. Their suffering disappears and their minds become peaceful, clear, and full of pure happiness. Wish them to have every good experience, from the satisfaction of ordinary needs and desires all the way to enlightenment. Concentrate on this feeling of love as long as possible.

Conclude the session by thinking that you definitely have the potential to love everyone, even those who annoy or hurt you, and those you don't even know. Generate a strong wish to work on your own anger, impatience, selfishness and the other problems that prevent you from having such love. Keeping your mind open and trying to overcome ego's prejudiced attitudes will leave much space in your heart for pure, universal love—and thus happiness for yourself and others—to develop.

Dedication Finally, dedicate the positive energy of your meditation to all beings, with the wish that they find happiness and enlightenment.

10

Meditation on Compassion and Tonglen (Giving and Taking)

onglen, which is Tibetan for "giving and taking," is a meditation for developing love and compassion. It is found in a series of teachings and practices known as thought transformation, or mind training (Tibetan: *lojong*). The idea behind these teachings is that we can transform our thoughts from being self-centered, deluded, and destructive to being loving, compassionate, and beneficial to others. Doing this is naturally good for others, but also for ourselves—we will feel more peaceful, happy, satisfied, and positive about ourselves. The ultimate goal of the practice is becoming enlightened, at which point we can make our existence as beneficial as possible for others.

One aspect of the thought transformation teachings is learning how to transform problems and difficulties into the spiritual path. Usually we dislike problems and do whatever we can to get rid of them as quickly as possible. But problems are not really problematic from their own side; it depends on how we view and deal with them. With the right understanding and methods we can make problems useful, in the same way that we recycle garbage or turn it into fertilizer for our garden.

For example, being stuck in a traffic jam is a problem if we let ourselves become impatient, thinking of all the things we'd rather be doing. But if we recognize the futility of such thoughts, and instead use the time to contemplate positive things, recite mantras, or listen to a spiritual teaching, then the situation becomes spiritual practice.

Tonglen is one such method for transforming problems. The basic idea of tonglen is that we meditate on love and compassion, generating the wish for others to be happy and free from suffering, and then we imagine *taking* on the suffering of others and *giving* them our happiness. People sometimes feel this way naturally—parents, for example, when they see their child suffering from illness, or rescue workers who are willing to risk their own lives to save those of others. But all of us can generate such courageous feelings by familiarizing ourselves with the meditations on love and compassion. It would also be helpful to have some familiarity with the meditation on emptiness, to lessen our habitual grasping at a real, permanent, independently-existing self.

In the full form of this meditation, we imagine taking on the suffering and causes of suffering—delusions and karma—of all living beings, and giving them all our happiness, wealth, good karma, etc. The practice is normally done in conjunction with breathing: while inhaling, we imagine taking in suffering and its causes, and these annihilate our selfishness and other delusions; and while exhaling, we imagine giving our happiness and goodness, and these become whatever others need to be happy and whole.

Initially, however, many people do not feel ready or able to take on the suffering of others. "I can't even handle my own problems; how can I take on everyone else's?" So it is advised that we first practice taking on our own suffering. When we become familiar and comfortable with that, we can then gradually take on the problems and suffering of others, starting with people we already love and care about, then strangers—people we are more distant from—and eventually even our "enemies."

The point of tonglen is not to focus on the feeling of *me* taking on suffering, and *me* giving away my happiness. Instead, we should focus on the *other people* becoming free of their suffering, and receiving all the happiness they need and wish for; and feel great joy and satisfaction that we have been able to bring this about. Also, the meditation involves *imagining* taking away others' suffering and giving them happiness; it's not possible to actually do that, except in very rare cases. So the purpose of the meditation is to train our mind in love, compassion, and bodhichitta, and to create the causes to become enlightened, at which point we will truly be able to help others be free of suffering and attain lasting peace and happiness.

Presented here are two simple versions of tonglen. The first involves taking on one of your own problems for the benefit of others, and is particularly helpful for those who do not feel ready to take on others' suffering. This meditation is very effective because a mistake we normally make is that when we have a problem we become obsessed with it, as if we were the only person in the world with such a problem; as if there was nothing else in the world, nothing positive, other than our problem. Such obsessive thinking makes a mountain out of a molehill. The problem may not be so bad, but our way of looking at it makes it seem immense, solid, and permanent, as if it will be there forever.

By recognizing that others have problems too, and that some have worse problems than ours, our problem will appear more like a molehill, more manageable. That itself gives a sense of relief, and the problem might even disappear altogether. But don't expect that! Expectations are obstacles to success in meditation. If nothing else, the meditation will open our heart and increase our compassion, our love, and our willingness to be more helpful to others.

The second version of tonglen involves taking on someone else's problem or suffering. You may wish to get accustomed to the first version before trying the second; you may feel comfortable to do both one after the other; or you may prefer to skip the first one and go straight to the second. There are no hard and fast rules—do whatever works best for you.

The practice

Sit comfortably with your back straight, and relax your body. Relax your mind by staying in the present, letting go of thoughts of the past, the future, other places, people, and so forth. Paying attention to the breath for several minutes will help your mind to settle in the here and now....

Motivation When your mind is more calm, generate a positive, altruistic motivation for doing the meditation. You can think, for example, "I am going to do this meditation in order to increase my positive feelings—compassion, love, and wanting to help others— so that my life and all the things I do will be only beneficial and never harmful to others."

Spend some time contemplating the following points to prepare your mind for the tonglen meditation:

All beings want to be happy. They have basic needs—for food, shelter, being comfortable, feeling safe and loved—and they have things they wish for—friends, possessions, a satisfying job, etc....
All beings also wish to be free of every kind of pain and problem....

Go into your heart, and get in touch with these basic feelings that we share with everyone else. Recognize that everything you do in your life is motivated by the wish to be happy and to avoid problems. The same is true for all other beings.... And don't feel that there is anything *wrong* with feeling this way—we all *deserve* to be happy and free from pain....

Then ask yourself: "If we are all the same in wanting to be peaceful, happy, and satisfied, and to not experience any unhappiness, pain, or problem, then is it right for me to care only for *my* happiness and *my* problems?"... And check: what is the result of such a self-centered attitude? Does it bring you the happiness you want, and prevent you from experiencing the problems you don't want?

Try to recognize that self-centeredness is counterproductive, and feel the wish to become less focused on yourself, and more loving and caring toward others. It *is* possible to transform your mind in this way, and one method that can help you to do this is the practice of tonglen....

Tonglen using one's own problem

Begin the tonglen practice by bringing to mind a problem that is currently troubling you. If you are not so familiar with this practice, it might be best to start with a small or medium-sized problem rather than your biggest one. It could be a physical problem—a painful or uncomfortable feeling, or an illness—or it could be something emotional, such as sadness, hurt, or loneliness. Allow the problem to arise in your mind, and feel how painful it is, how your mind wants to push it away....

Then think: "I am not the only person in the world experiencing a problem like this. There are many others...." Think of other people who may be experiencing the same or a similar problem, some to an even greater degree than yourself. (For example, if you have lost a loved one, think of people who have lost many loved ones, in a war or natural disaster.) Generate compassion for them, thinking, and really *feeling:* "How wonderful it would be if all those people could be free from their suffering."

Then decide that you will accept or take on your own experience of this problem with the compassionate wish that by doing so, all those other people will be free from their suffering. Let go of your resistance, fear, and aversion toward your problem, and allow your mind to rest in a gentle, peaceful acceptance of it....

When you are more familiar and comfortable with this practice, you can use it to take on bigger problems you have at present, and also the problems you will probably experience in the future.

Tonglen for another person's problem

Imagine in front of you someone you know and love who is suffering. Put yourself in their situation, and try to really feel the suffering they are experiencing and how they wish to be free of it.... Feel how wonderful it would be if they *could* be free from all their suffering and problems. Then generate the courage to take their suffering upon yourself.

Visualize that your delusions such as self-centeredness, anger, attachment, and jealousy are in the form of a solid, dark rock in your heart. Then visualize your loved one's suffering in the form of thick, dark smoke floating out of their body. As you inhale, imagine taking this dark smoke of suffering into yourself. It comes to your heart, absorbs into the rock of self-centeredness and delusions, and destroys it. Both the rock and the suffering, your own and that of the other person, become utterly non-existent. Feel a sense of joy that this person is now free from his or her suffering and problems....

When you exhale, breathe out your happiness, positive qualities, and merit in the form of bright light. Imagine that it transforms into whatever will bring joy and peace of mind to this person: material things, love and friendship, inner qualities such as love, compassion, courage, and equanimity. Imagine that their needs and wishes are fulfilled, their mind is filled with peace, happiness, and all the knowledge and qualities of the spiritual path. Let your mind rest for some time in a feeling of joyfulness that you have been able to help your loved one in this way.

As you become more familiar with this meditation, you can practice it gradually with more of your friends and relatives, then strangers, and eventually even with those you dislike.

Dedication When you wish to conclude the meditation, remember the motivation you started with, and dedicate the positive energy of doing the meditation to the happiness and enlightenment of all beings. (For another meditation on thought transformation, see page 200.)

11
Dealing with Negative Energy

As mindfulness develops we become increasingly sensitive to our thoughts and feelings, including negative states of mind such as anger, irritation, pride, depression, desire, and so forth. Why are these considered "negative"? It is not that anger or desire are inherently evil or that we should feel ashamed when they arise. They are negative because they are delusions—distorted conceptions that paint a false picture of reality—and because they lead to unhappiness, confusion, and problems. But with the right understanding and the right tools, every experience that arises in our mind, negative as well as positive, can be a constructive step on the path.

The root cause of negative emotions is the false notion of inherent, graspable, solid existence that we impute onto everything. This misconception gives rise to *attachment* to whatever appears pleasant, *aversion* or *anger* toward whatever is unpleasant or painful, and an uncaring *ignorance* about everything else. Thus our mind divides everyone and everything in the world around us into *friend, enemy,* and *stranger.* And these three mental toxins in turn branch out into all our other negative states of mind.

However, like all your experiences, negative emotions are impermanent, neither fixed nor concrete. They are simply mental energy, like love and joy, whose nature is clear and nonmaterial. Sometimes you might feel overwhelmed by them and doubt whether you can ever control your mind at all. But don't worry. Delusions come and go in your mind; they are not *you.*

Usually we either completely identify with our anger, for example, without any clarity or understanding at all, or suppress it altogether, refusing to acknowledge what is going on. Both approaches—getting caught up in the emotion, or suppressing it—are unskillful and only make matters worse.

A more skillful approach is to honestly acknowledge the presence of the emotion, but step back and observe it in a detached way within the calm spaciousness of meditation. With mindfulness and awareness of its nature—how it is just a momentary experience in our mind, not something solid and fixed, and not *me*—we may be able to just let go of it, and let it pass out of our mind.

But "letting go" is not always easy, especially if the emotion is habitual or very strong. If that is the case, then we can use one or more of the methods explained below to analyze the emotion to see how it is mistaken, and to transform our mental state into one that is more realistic and positive. Dealing with anger or any other negative emotion in this way becomes a beneficial, learning experience.

But for some people, or for some problems, it may be difficult to "be your own therapist." Analyzing and transforming a powerful emotion such as anger requires a fair amount of skill and wisdom. So if you find this difficult to do on your own, you may want to seek help from a spiritual teacher, a good therapist, or a wise, caring friend. No one else can change your mind—that is something only you can do—but talking with others can give you some new, helpful ideas and perspectives to work with.

The methods explained in this chapter are practical ways of dealing with *attachment, anger, depression,* and *fear*. An important first step in working with emotions is recognizing and identifying them. Sometimes our mind is like a thick jungle of disturbing thoughts and emotions; it's hard to really see what's going on. With mindfulness, honesty, and discriminating intelligence we can start to identify what's what: "That's anger; that's desire; that's fear;" and so on. Once we know what we're up against, we can choose the appropriate methods.

The second step is having a healthy, balanced attitude toward the negative emotions. Attitudes to avoid include guilt; self-hatred or self-judgment; and identifying with the emotion, for example "*I am* my anger," which leads us to be obsessed and act it out. We can avoid these by remembering that delusions are impermanent, coming and going in our mind like clouds in the sky, and that they are not our true nature. The real nature of the mind is pure, free of delusions, like a clear, cloudless sky.

The next step is to work on the delusions in meditation, using one or more antidotes. If there are a number of different emotions disturbing your mind at the same time, it's best to start with the one that is strongest and most troublesome—don't try to take them all on at once! Once you've managed to get the biggest one a bit more under control, then you can move on to the next biggest.

Some of the methods explained here provide new ways of looking at these emotions, while others present new ways of looking at the object or situation we're feeling emotional about. They are not magical solutions to what are, after all, difficult problems. Dealing with negative energy is hard work, but with practice and patience it is possible to gradually change our attitudes as a first step to changing our actual experience of people and situations. If we become familiar with these methods in meditation it will be easier to apply them spontaneously when the need arises.

Begin every meditation session with a positive, altruistic motivation, then spend some time observing your breath to bring your mind to a calm state within which you can reflect objectively on your negative emotions and the antidotes to them.

Attachment

To want something and not want to be separated from it: very broadly, this is attachment, also known as desire. Attendant to it is the false assumption that having whatever it is we want will bring satisfaction: this is why attachment causes problems.

Attachment is difficult to detect and even more difficult to find fault with; we think it is the road to happiness and satisfaction.

But fulfillment of desire is an illusion; desire leads to more desire, not satisfaction.

We may be able to see how attachment to alcohol, drugs, or money leads to problems rather than happiness, but we may wonder what is wrong with attachment to people. Wouldn't life be empty and meaningless without family and friends?

This question arises because we confuse attachment with love. Attachment is concerned with *my* needs, *my* happiness, while love is an unselfish attitude, concerned with the needs and happiness of others. Most of the time our love is mixed with attachment because we do not feel adequate or secure on our own, and try to find wholeness through another. But when a relationship involves attachment, problems inevitably arise. We become dependent on the good feelings and comfort of the relationship and then suffer when it changes. Real, lasting happiness can only be found within ourselves, and we will never find it as long as we lean helplessly on others. A relationship free of unrealistic grasping is free of disappointment, conflict, jealousy, and other problems, and is fertile ground for the growth of love and wisdom.

Overcoming attachment does not mean becoming cold and indifferent. On the contrary, detachment means learning to have relaxed control over our mind through understanding the real causes of happiness and fulfillment, and this enables us to enjoy life more and suffer less.

Ways to deal with attachment

1. Contemplate the faults of attachment. Examine carefully the mind that experiences it. It is excited and full of unrealistic expectations. It glosses over the facts and deals with projected fantasies. It cannot see things clearly and is unable to make intelligent judgments. Is this happiness?

Also, the consequences of attachment are not peace and satisfaction, but disappointment and desire for more of the same. Think of the suffering you experience when you separate from an object of attachment. We all know the pain of relationships that did not work and the grief over a loved one's death.

Recognize that attachment is not a peaceful, clear state of mind, and that it leads to dissatisfaction and unhappiness. And making a habit of it leaves on our mindstream imprints to experience more problems in the future.

Attachment clouds the mind and prevents us from recognizing its faults. It is very important to be honest with ourselves, to penetrate attachment's facade and analyze its real nature.

2. Recall that all things are impermanent. By their nature they change from moment to moment and will inevitably perish. The object of your attachment will not always be attractive and pleasing; visualize it as old, faded, and worn and then check if your feelings about it remain the same. And how would you feel if you lost it altogether?

The pleasure you experience is impermanent, too. For how long do you really feel pleased and satisfied with any one object?

When we recognize that external things cannot give us lasting happiness and satisfaction, our attachment to them will lessen— and we'll probably enjoy them all the more!

3. Meditate on death. Remember the inevitability of death and that it could come at any time. Imagine how you will feel about separating forever from your objects of attachment: loved ones, enjoyments, possessions. Not only are they unable to help you as you die, but your attachment to them will upset your mind and hinder a peaceful death.

4. The best remedy to attachment and all other delusions is to think about emptiness. Investigate the I that experiences the attachment. What is its nature? Try to locate this seemingly real, solid I in your body or mind.

Examine also the object of attachment. Is this person or thing inherently wonderful and pleasing? If so, why doesn't everyone appreciate it? Can you see how your mind exaggerates and gets excited about the object?

Try to see that both the I and its object are empty of inherent existence; they do not exist in the way they appear: in and of themselves. This might sound pretty unconvincing—especially when attachment is strong—but consider it carefully. Just thinking about emptiness is useful and helps us to gradually understand what it means, and to loosen the grasp of our attachment.

5. If you feel strongly attached to an attractive body (including your own), think about it in the following way.

First, analyze just what it is you find so attractive. Then mentally penetrate the surface and examine what lies beneath the skin: the flesh, bones, blood vessels, and organs. Visualize the mucus, pus, blood, excrement, and urine. Imagine it all in vivid detail. What is it you find so attractive here?

Imagine the body old, bent, and wrinkled: where is the beautiful body now?

The point of this exercise is not to go to the other extreme and dislike yourself or the person you're attracted to. Rather it is to see how attachment distorts our perception and exaggerates the qualities of a person or thing. We simply don't see reality as it is. This analysis, therefore, brings us down to earth and helps us penetrate below the surface of our glossy fantasy image.

6. A remedy for attachment to food is to contemplate the suffering experienced by all the beings involved in its preparation. Animals are killed to provide us with meat and fish; innumerable small animals and insects are killed in the cultivation, fertilization, and spraying of the grains, fruit, and vegetables that we eat. Recall the hard work of the farmers, fishermen, fruitpickers, factory workers, truck drivers, shop assistants, and cooks.

Try to eat mindfully, with appreciation for all these beings' kindness and sacrifice.

Anger

As opposed to attachment—wanting not to be separated from something or someone—anger is the attitude of wanting to be separated; of wanting to harm. Most of our anger is directed toward other people, but we can also be angry at ourselves or at inanimate objects. Anger ranges from a feeling of irritation about the way someone drinks tea, for example, to the powerful hatred that leads to physical violence or murder. It is usually related to attachment. As one teacher has pointed out, anger is the response when attachment doesn't get what it wants.

Anger is the very opposite of patience, tolerance, compassion, and love. It is a distorted conception, a mistaken way of reacting to things, a delusion, and brings only problems and unhappiness, not the results we want. It disturbs our mind and causes us to hurt others through our actions and words, and is not an intelligent, skillful way to react, in any situation.

Patience, the opposite of anger, is a very beneficial state of mind because it enables us to accept difficulties with a minimum of suffering. But patience has to be learned, and the way to develop it is by practicing the remedies to anger.

The faults of anger are much easier to recognize than those of attachment; nevertheless, anger is very difficult to deal with. Part of the problem is our unwillingness even to admit that we have it, or, if we do recognize our anger, to admit that it is a fault. We may want to be peaceful and kind, but in our efforts we probably suppress feelings of dislike, annoyance, and resentment, the more subtle aspects of anger. This is no solution. The emotions are still there, brewing below the surface of our mind, making us tense and nervous, and affecting other people.

Another mistaken approach is to see anger as a natural energy that should not be restrained but expressed whenever it arises. This may well relieve us of the immediate tension of our emotions and thus appear to be a skillful way of handling anger, but again it is no solution. We need only look at the short-term effects—how it disturbs ourselves and others—and the long-term—becoming habitually angry—to see that it is not at all useful or intelligent to give in to anger.

The truly skillful approach is to recognize the anger or irritation as it arises, keep it within our mind and deal with it there. Catching it, when we first feel it, is itself enough to defuse much of the anger-energy. Then we should examine the emotion from many angles: what are its causes? What do we hope to achieve by it? How do we view the situation? Having a clear understanding of anger gives us a firmer hold on it, because when we see how unreasonable it is, we are less likely to get involved in it.

Anger distorts our view of things. So after examining it we should apply an antidote, such as òne of the methods below, in order to bring our mind around to a more correct, realistic view. However, this is not easy. The energy of anger is very powerful, and we are not in the habit of trying to control or transform it. It is useful to use these methods over and over again in meditation, working with past experiences of anger or imagined situations; then, when anger occurs in our day-to-day relationships, we can bring to mind whatever insights we have developed in our practice sessions and try to avoid following the old familiar route of getting angry.

We won't always be successful, of course. Sometimes minutes, hours, or days go by before we even realize that we got angry and hurt someone! But it is never too late to do something about it. Sit down, recall the situation, recognize what went wrong and figure out how to avoid the same mistakes again. We can also do a purification practice to remedy the karma created, and apologize to the person we hurt.

The same practices can be done to resolve problems we had years before. There is no reason to feel discouraged if anger continues to arise strongly; it takes time to break powerful habits. The important thing is to *want* and *try* to work on it.

Ways to deal with anger

1. Contemplate the faults or disadvantages of anger, so that you become convinced that it's harmful rather than helpful, and therefore not something you want to indulge in. First of all, look at the immediate effects of anger on your mind and body. What is it like being angry? Is your mind peaceful and happy, or disturbed and discontented? Are you able to think clearly and make intelligent decisions, or does your thinking become confused and irrational?

And how does it affect your body? Do you feel calm and relaxed, or agitated and tense? Scientific studies have shown that anger is a significant cause of certain health problems, such as heart disease and cancer, as well as of premature death.

How does your anger affect the people around you? If you express your anger in words and actions, what is the result? It may cause you to hurt people you love and damage cherished relationships. But even the anger directed at your "enemies"—those who you think deserve to be hurt—may come back at you later. So is that the wisest way of dealing with them?

There are more subtle, less obvious, effects of anger on our psyche. In terms of karma, getting angry leaves imprints on our mind that will bring painful experiences in the future—more suffering. And it destroys much of the good karma that we have worked so hard to accumulate. It is a major obstacle to the cultivation of positive qualities such as love, compassion, and wisdom, and to making progress on the spiritual path....

Recognize the harmful results of anger, resolve not to let your mind be taken over by it, and instead learn ways of defusing it.

2. Remember karma, cause and effect (see page 80). If someone harms you in some way—by being abusive or unfriendly, cheating or stealing from you, or wrecking your belongings—and it seems you have done nothing to deserve it, check again.

According to Buddhism, any misfortune that comes our way is the result of harmful actions we created in the past—in this or other lives. We reap what we have sown. When we can see our problems in this light, we will be better able to accept and take responsibility for them rather than dump the blame on others. Also, if we understand that getting angry and retaliating will just bring us more problems in the future, we'll resolve to be more patient, and more careful about the karma we create.

3. Another method for dealing with people who hurt or annoy you is to put yourself in their place and try to see the situation from their point of view. What is driving them to behave in this way? Is their state of mind peaceful and happy, or confused, miserable, and uncontrolled? They are human just like you, with problems

and worries, trying to be happy and make the best of life. Recall your own experiences of being angry and unkind to get a better idea of what they are going through.

Also, consider what the outcome will be if they continue to act in deluded ways. Will they be happy and satisfied, or are they just creating more trouble and suffering for themselves? If we really understand others' confusion and pain, we'll be less likely to react with anger—which would just give them even more suffering—and more likely to regard them with compassion.

4. The Buddhist teachings say that we would not see faults in others if we did not have those faults in ourselves—as the saying goes, "it takes one to know one." Other people are therefore like mirrors, showing us what we need to work on in ourselves.

Check exactly what it is that you dislike or are angry at in the other person. Then look into yourself and see if you can find the same thing, or something similar. It may be obvious: you might easily remember having done the same thing yourself, or realize you have the same bad habit.

But in some cases you may need to look deeper—it could be a quality you have long suppressed, regarding it as wrong and unacceptable. And that is where the problem lies: because you don't accept that part of yourself, you cannot accept it in others and so you feel angry when you see it.

The solution is to learn to accept that behavior or quality in yourself. "Accepting" doesn't mean condoning it, and thinking you can be that way all you want. It means being honest and acknowledging the existence of that fault, but at the same time knowing you can work on decreasing and eventually overcoming it. Being more accepting and compassionate about our own shortcomings will enable us to be more accepting and compassionate toward others.

5. Anger is more likely to arise in our mind when we are unhappy or dissatisfied. If you notice yourself getting irritated and angry about even small things, sit down and check what's going on in the deeper levels of your mind. Are you feeling dissatisfied about

something? Are there unhappy, critical thoughts about yourself or aspects of your life? Are you focusing more on the negative side of things rather than the positive side? If this is the case, the meditation on appreciating your human life (page 59) is a good remedy for this. There *are* good things about yourself and your life, and if you pay more attention to these, your mind will be happier and more satisfied, and you will be less likely to react with anger, even when bigger problems occur.

6. When anger arises, turn your attention within and investigate the I that is angry. Analyze where and how it exists. Apply whatever understanding of emptiness you have.

Investigate the object of your anger also. Does it exist in the solid and definite way that it appears to you? If the person you are angry at is really so bad and unlikable from their own side, independent of how your mind perceives them, then they would appear that way to everyone. Is that true, or are there people who like and admire that person?

Try to see that the situation is like a dream: although it seems very real at the moment, from your point of view at a later time, even tomorrow, it will appear distant and faded, a mere memory.

7. Difficult situations are usually the most productive in terms of spiritual growth. Thus someone who arouses our anger is giving us a chance to learn that we still have work to do.

We might think we've come a long way in understanding and controlling our mind and that we are fairly peaceful now—but, all of a sudden, anger arises! It follows, then, that when people make us angry, they are giving us the chance to see where we are at, and to put our knowledge to use and increase our patience. Contemplate this and strengthen your determination to understand your anger, bring it under control and learn to react instead with patience. It will benefit yourself and others.

8. Contemplate the points of the death meditation. Death could happen at any time, so realize that it is senseless to cling to dif-

ferences with people. Dying with unresolved anger creates havoc in your mind and makes a peaceful death impossible.

The other person could die at any time too. How would you feel if this happened before you were able to clear up the problems between you?

You, the other person, and your interaction will all definitely come to an end. Seen in this light, are the problems really so important? Are they worth the anguish and unhappiness they cause?

9. Having gained some control over your anger through one of these methods, you might like to work on developing love. You can do this by practicing the meditation on love, visualizing in front of you the person who makes you angry and making a special effort to actually reverse your feelings for them.

10. All the methods explained above involve meditating to try to deal with anger on our own; it is also possible to resolve a conflict by communicating with the other person. But here we have to be careful. First of all we have to consider whether or not the other person would be open to such communication and if it would bring positive results. Second we should check our motivation very carefully: do we really want to straighten out our differences with this person and come to a better mutual understanding, or do we just want to express how irritated we are or win a victory?

If we start discussing the problem with the desire to hurt or with expectations and demands, the communication will not work. So we need to be very clear about our intentions and very sincere and honest in explaining our feelings. This kind of open communication is very powerful and can transform enemies into friends.

Of course, sometimes anger is very strong and the last thing you feel like doing is sitting down to meditate! At least you should try to avoid getting totally involved and speaking angrily or becoming violent. You can try some method for releasing your energy without harming the person, or become completely unresponsive, like stone or wood, until your anger has cooled down. Later, when your mind is more calm, you can meditate on the problem and apply one of the antidotes.

A frequently recurring problem, like getting angry at someone you live or work with, can be handled more effectively if you think about the situation in meditation and plan what to say and do when it next occurs. Then you will be better prepared and less likely to be caught off-guard.

Depression

There are various forms of depression. Some are short-term and occur due to problems such as loss, illness, or not getting something we want; others are long-term and may be caused by genetic or biological factors. Meditation can be helpful for at least some cases of depression; however, those that are severe or long-term may require medical or therapeutic treatment.

Depression is a dark, heavy, unhappy state of mind, self-centered and lacking in positive energy. It frequently involves self-hatred, self-criticism, or other negative thought-patterns. It is unrealistic, exaggerating the negative side of things and ignoring the positive side; seeing the glass as half empty rather than half full.

Depression usually focuses on *my* problem and blows it up out of proportion. Our thoughts spiral downward; we feel the situation is hopeless with no possibility of improving. We feel sorry for ourselves, seeing our ego at the center of a sad story, and we have little or no energy to share with others. We find it difficult to take care of ourselves, and we may bring others down with us.

We all have the tendency to be depressed at times. We are not perfect, and life doesn't always go smoothly. We make mistakes, and we don't have control over what comes our way. When we are unable to accept these problems cheerfully as natural aspects of life or to deal with them skillfully, we become depressed. Of course, the pain we experience is real and the problems need to be taken care of. But sinking into depression is not the answer—it only deepens and complicates our unhappiness. The best solution is to analyze our thought patterns to see how we interpret the situation and try to recognize where we go wrong. Gradually we can learn to catch ourselves in time; to look at things more positively and to use our natural wisdom.

Ways to deal with depression

1. Take a step back from your thoughts and feelings and check what they are saying. Depression often involves repetitive, self-critical thoughts such as "I'm worthless;" "Nobody cares about me;" "I never do anything right." If we are honest with ourselves, we'll recognize that these thoughts are mistaken or exaggerated, focusing on the negative and ignoring the positive.

If you can, then do the meditation on appreciating your human life. Even if your problem is a very serious one, it is important to remember that you have much positive energy and great potential. It is always possible to overcome (or at least lighten) depression by changing your way of thinking, by emphasizing the positive rather than the negative aspects of your personality and your life; they *do* exist! It's all a matter of you seeing and identifying with them rather than with your depressed, low view of yourself.

You can then "change the tape" by bringing into your mind more realistic, positive thoughts such as "I have such-and-such good qualities;" "There *are* people who love and care about me;" "I *can do* this-and-that well." You can even feel good about the fact that you are still alive—you haven't yet died from illness, an accident, or a natural disaster—and about all the things you can do with your body and mind.

2. Meditate on the clarity of your mind. Your unhappiness, worry, and frustration, as well as your good feelings, are all just mental energy—clear, non-physical, and transitory. Simply observe the different thoughts and experiences that pass through your mind, without judging them or getting involved in them.

Remember that all experiences are impermanent. You may have felt depressed in the past, but where is that experience now? It's gone. The same will happen with your present depression. It may last a few hours or days, but eventually it will disappear. And even within that time it is not constant. If you observe your mind carefully, you will notice moments of lightness or joy interspersed with moments of sadness. Do not cling to any of these but let them go.

Remember that your mind is a stream of different experiences—joyful, unhappy, positive, negative—all of the same clear, immaterial nature. These experiences appear and dissolve like waves on the ocean, lasting only a short time. Your depression is like a wave: a transient, ephemeral experience, so it is not appropriate to cling to it, thinking, "This is me."

3. Investigate the I (see page 53), your sense of self that identifies strongly with unhappy thoughts and feelings. Try to find this I. What is its nature? Is it part of your body or your mind, or is it somewhere else? Is this depressed I something permanent, solid, unchanging?

4. Meditate on love (page 111), or compassion and tonglen (page 116). Turning outward toward others and contemplating their needs and suffering will help you be less self-centered and thus see your problems more realistically. However, take care when contemplating suffering—if it causes you to feel more depressed, then back off and switch to something positive and uplifting.

5. Do one of the visualization meditations (part 5), for example, the body of light, Tara, or purification meditations. These can be very quick ways to cut through your depressed view of things.

6. A very effective remedy for depression is to get out and help others: do some volunteer or service work. This has been found to cause the release of endorphins—the "happy hormones"—in our nervous system, so we naturally feel better. Doing physical exercise has the same effect. These methods can be useful at times when we're too depressed to meditate!

Fear

In traditional Buddhist explanations of the delusions, or disturbing emotions, fear is not usually mentioned, but it is a common cause of unhappiness and stress. Fear is not necessarily negative; it depends on what we're afraid of and how we handle our fears. It can in fact be useful in our everyday life as well as in our spiritual practice. Fear of hurting ourselves and others in a car accident motivates us to drive carefully and observe the rules of the road; fear of disease and an early death motivates us to eat wisely and take care of our health; fear of a negative, out-of-control state of mind at the time of death motivates us to prepare ourselves for death by developing a spiritual practice; fear of the painful consequences of negative actions motivates us to refrain from creating bad karma and act compassionately.

Nevertheless, fear can bring negative results. It disturbs our peace of mind, it can harm our health, it causes us to see things in a mistaken way, and it can motivate us to act irrationally or destructively, so it *is* something we should aim to overcome. One of the qualities of an enlightened mind is being free of all fears.

The root cause of fear and anxiety is our misconception of our "I" and all other things, seeing them as solid, real, and permanent. From this arises attachment to whoever or whatever appears pleasant and helpful, and fear of separating from or losing them. Toward the people, things, and experiences we see as unpleasant or unwanted, we feel aversion and fear of *not* separating from them.

We rarely face our fears to try to understand and deal with them skillfully. We may feel overwhelmed by them, or helpless, not knowing how to deal with them. Or we may suppress them, thinking, "Fear is bad; I shouldn't be afraid," or "If I ignore it, it will go away." But this is not the way to become free of fear; instead, our fears remain in our subconscious, subtly affecting our thoughts and feelings, and our life.

The methods below show us how we can start to face our fears, analyze them to understand what they're about, and change our attitudes.

Ways to deal with fear

1. Look at your fear. Sit down and make your mind calm with some breathing meditation. Then allow the fear to come into the clear spaciousness of your mind. Don't let yourself get caught up in it, but stand back and examine it objectively. Ask yourself, what exactly is it that I'm afraid of?

Then ask yourself: Is it reasonable for me to have this fear? Is it likely that what I'm afraid of will actually happen, or is my mind getting carried away with highly unrealistic fantasies?

If it *is* possible that it will happen, then is there anything you can do to prevent or avoid it? If so, decide to do it, and stop worrying!

If there's nothing you can do, or even if you try to prevent it, it might happen anyway, then are there things you can do to prepare yourself for that? Think of other people who have been through that experience. See if you can draw strength from that awareness: if they could do it, so can I.

It's good to keep in mind the advice of the great Indian master Santideva: "Why be unhappy (or worried) about something if it can be remedied? And what is the use of being unhappy (or worried) about something if it cannot be remedied?" In other words, if there's something that can be done to prevent or remedy an unwanted situation, we should do it, but if there's nothing that can be done, it's useless to worry; better to just accept it!

2. If you are afraid of change, loss, or death, you can meditate on impermanence and death. Familiarizing ourselves with the reality of how we, others, and the things in the world around us are changing all the time and will eventually disappear enables us to gradually become more accepting and less fearful.

3. Contemplate how it's in the nature of unenlightened existence to encounter problems and painful, undesirable experiences (see the meditation on suffering, page 97). This is true for you, and it's true for all other unenlightened beings—you are not alone! But this situation will not last forever. You and everyone else have the potential to be free of all suffering, and to experience perfect

peace and happiness forever. Problems occur because of causes and conditions—primarily karma and delusions—and these can definitely be eliminated. Resolve to apply your energy to the work of refraining from negative actions, purifying those you have already created, doing as many positive actions as possible, and working on your mind to overcome the delusions which are the main cause of suffering.

4. The Dalai Lama often says that a very effective way to instill courage and confidence in yourself is to generate an altruistic motivation for the things you do. For example, if you're feeling nervous about talking to a large group of people—or even to one person!—spend some time beforehand contemplating love, compassion, and the sincere wish to benefit others. Filling your mind with concern for others leaves little or no space for egotistical worries like "will they like *me*?" or "what will happen to *me*?" so the communication will probably be more successful and satisfying. And even if the outcome is not quite what we hoped for, at least we can feel good about the fact that we acted with an altruistic motivation rather than a self-centered one.

5. Since the root of fear is our mistaken conception of the way we and everyone and everything else exists, it's useful to meditate on emptiness. When you feel fear, go within and examine the I that is frightened. Is it something real, existing from its own side? If so, where and how does it exist—in my body? In my mind?

You can also do the same analysis on the thing you are frightened of, to see if it exists in the solid, real way that it appears to your mind.

6. Some people find it helpful to bring to mind an object of refuge when they feel frightened. For Buddhists, this could be the Buddha, or another enlightened being such as Avalokiteshvara (page 155), or Tara (page 151), who is actually renowned for relieving people of all kinds of fears. There are many stories of people experiencing amazing results by praying to or reciting the mantras of these holy

beings. But even if nothing amazing happens outside of us, taking refuge and praying helps us to feel more calm and courageous inside, and better able to handle the difficult situation we are in.

Part Five

VISUALIZATION
MEDITATIONS

About Visualization

In your attempts to calm and concentrate your mind, you have probably noticed visual images among the many things that distract your attention from the object of meditation: faces of loved ones, your home, other familiar places, appetizing food, or memories of films you have seen. Such images arise spontaneously throughout the day but we are often too engrossed in external sensations to notice them. And every night our mind creates vivid scenes in which we interact with dream-people and dream-events. Visualization, or imagination, is thus a mental technique we are all familiar with—in fact, we probably visualize all the time—but unless our work lies in, say, art, design, or film, we do little or nothing to develop and utilize it.

This natural capacity to think in pictures can be used to deepen our meditative experiences. Visualization is used in several ways in the Tibetan tradition of spiritual development. It adds another dimension to analytical meditations—for example, visualizing ourselves dying sharpens the awareness of our mortality, and visualizing actual people while meditating on love and compassion makes the cultivation of those qualities more authentic and heartfelt. A mental image of the Buddha is recommended as the focus of attention in the development of single-pointed concentration, and visualizing enlightened beings while praying helps to enhance our faith and conviction.

But the art of visualization is used to the fullest in Vajrayana or tantra, the most profound and rapid means of reaching enlightenment. The practices of this path involve identifying oneself completely, body and mind, with an enlightened being and seeing one's environment as a pure realm. The ordinary, mistaken perceptions of oneself and all other phenomena are thus gradually abandoned as one's potential for enlightenment is allowed to express itself.

The buddhas visualized in Vajrayana practice, such as Tara and Avalokiteshvara, are symbols of the enlightened state. Each is a manifestation of a specific quality—Avalokiteshvara, for example, is the buddha of compassion—but each also represents the total experience of enlightenment. The details of the visualization, such as colors, implements, hand gestures, posture, and so forth, symbolize different aspects of the path to spiritual fulfillment.

Meditation on these buddhas (or images from other traditions that you are more comfortable with, for example Christ or Mary) helps us to open our hearts to the pure energies of love, compassion, wisdom, and strength that are ever-present, all around us, wherever we may be. And, as the potential for these enlightened qualities lies within us, we should consider the images we contemplate to be reflections of our own true nature. Although ultimate reality is inexpressible, words lead us to discover it; so too can images remind us of the experience of enlightenment until it becomes a living reality.

The two kinds of meditation—analytical and stabilizing—are used together in visualization techniques. We need analytical thought to construct the image at the beginning of the meditation and to recall it whenever it is lost during the session. Analysis is also used to deal with other problems that might occur, such as distraction or negative thoughts.

But developing a clear visualization depends primarily on stabilizing meditation. Once the image has been established and we feel comfortable with it, we should hold it with single-pointed attention, not letting our mind be distracted by other objects. Initially, our concentration will last only a few seconds, but with continual practice we will be able to maintain it for increasingly longer periods of time. Every time our attention wanders or we lose the object, we should again bring it to mind. This way of meditating both increases our familiarity with positive images and strengthens our ability to control and concentrate the mind.

It is common to find visualization difficult. If you are having problems, it could be that you are trying too hard or expecting too much. The mind needs to be in the right state—relaxed, clear, and open. Too much effort creates tension, and then the only vision that can appear is darkness. Too little concentration means the mind is crowded with distractions, leaving no space for a visualized image. We should learn to adjust our concentration as we would tune a musical instrument—with sensitivity and patience—until we have found the proper mental state in which the object can appear clearly.

Remember too that visualization utilizes only the *mental* faculty, not the eyes. If you find that you are straining to see something, you misunderstand the technique. Relax and let the image appear from within your mind.

Furthermore, we should be satisfied with whatever does appear, even if it is just a partial image, or a blur of color, or nothing at all! The important thing is feeling the *presence* of an enlightened being, rather than being concerned about having a perfect visualization. Thus it is very important to be relaxed and free of expectations, and feel confident that the buddha is there. It is self-defeating to expect a complete, perfect visualization after one or two attempts; it may take years of practice before you can really see the image. Again, it is a matter of tuning the mind to the right balance; learning to work with the energies and elements of the mind to produce a positive, joyful meditative experience.

You might find it useful to practice visualization with familiar objects. Sit quietly with your eyes closed and bring to mind the image of a friend, for example. Try to see the details: the color and shape of the eyes, nose, and mouth, the style of the hair, the shape of the body, and so forth. Experiment with other objects: your house, the view from your window, even your own face.

Visualizing buddhas is made easier by gazing at a picture or statue, then closing your eyes and trying to recall the image in detail. However, this helps you with the details only; don't think your visualized figure should be flat like a drawing or cold and lifeless like a statue. It should be warm, full of life and feeling, three-dimensional, and made of pure, radiant light. Feel that you are actually in the presence of a blissful, compassionate, enlightened being.

Finally, it might be useful to practice the following simple visualization before attempting more complicated techniques.

1

Body of Light Meditation

Motivation Sit comfortably, with your back straight, and breathe naturally. Generate a positive, beneficial motivation for doing the meditation, then spend some time observing the natural rhythm of your breathing to settle your mind.

When your mind is calm and clear, visualize in the space above your head a sphere of white light, somewhat smaller than the size of your head, and pure, transparent, nonmaterial. Spend several minutes concentrating on the presence of the light. Don't worry if it does not appear sharply; it is enough just to feel it is there.

Think that the sphere of light represents all universal goodness, love, and wisdom: the fulfillment of your own highest potential. Then visualize that it decreases in size until it is about one inch in diameter and descends through the top of your head to your heart-center. From there it begins to expand once more, slowly spreading to fill your entire body. As it does, all the solid parts of your body dissolve and become light—your organs, bones, blood vessels, tissues, and skin all become pure, translucent white light.

Concentrate on the experience of your body as a body of light. Think that all problems, negativities, and hindrances have completely vanished, and that you have reached a state of wholeness and perfection. Feel serene and joyful. If any thought or distracting object should appear in your mind, let it also dissolve into white light. Meditate in this way for as long as you can.

Dedication Finish by dedicating the positive energy of the meditation to the benefit of all beings.

2
Simple Purification Meditation

There are both positive and negative aspects to our personality. On the one hand we have love, wisdom, joy, and generosity, but on the other we have anger, selfishness, laziness, and a long list of other problems. All these traits are just mental experiences, waves on the ocean of our consciousness; all have the same basic, clear nature. They are not static and permanent but constantly in flux, coming and going.

There are, however, two important distinctions to be made: positive states of mind are productive, beneficial for ourselves and others, whereas negative states are harmful and bring only confusion and pain. Peace of mind is achieved by cultivating what is positive and abandoning what is negative.

The second point is that anger and the other mental disorders arise from our misconceptions about the way things exist, while positive states of mind are realistic and arise from right understanding. When we recognize this and develop a correct view of reality, our negativities gradually lessen and eventually disappear altogether. As our wisdom develops, our spontaneous good feelings grow and our personality gradually transforms. At the end of this path is enlightenment, the perfection of all beneficial qualities—a state of great clarity and loving compassion.

Often we identify ourselves more with our negative side than our positive side, and feel guilty about mistakes we have made. We believe, "I am hopeless; I can't control my anger; I don't do anything right; I'm completely cold and unable to love anyone." Although we may have faults and problems, it is wrong to think that they are permanent. We *can* free ourselves from negative energy and the burden of guilt, as long as we are willing to work. One way of doing this is through the process of purification.

Purification is a recurring theme in Buddhist meditation. It is chiefly a question of changing our way of thinking. When we think we are impure and negative, we become just that. A low, depressed self-image gradually permeates our behavior and outlook on life. We feel limited and inadequate and don't even give ourselves a chance to change. But, by recognizing our potential for perfection and sincerely putting energy into developing it, we cultivate a more positive self-image. Believing that we are basically pure is the first step in *becoming* pure. What needs to be purified, therefore, is our lack of self-confidence and tendency to identify with our negative energy, as well as the negative energy itself.

This simplified meditation contains the essence of purification: letting go of problems and mistakes, and seeing them as temporary obscurations rather than an intrinsic part of our nature. It helps us to get in touch with and develop our natural good energy.

The practice

Be comfortable and relaxed. Take a few minutes to settle your mind in the here and now.

Motivation Bring to mind a beneficial reason as your motivation for doing the meditation, such as wishing to become more free from negative energy so that you can be more helpful and less harmful to others.

Turn your attention to your breath. Breathe normally and observe the full duration of every inhalation and exhalation.

When your mind is calm, imagine that when you inhale, all the positive energy in the universe enters your body in the form of pure, blissful, radiant white light. Visualize this light flowing to every part of your body, filling every cell and atom, and making you relaxed, light, and blissful. Do this visualization with every inhalation.

Once you are familiar and comfortable with breathing in the white light, then begin to breathe out dark smoke with every exhalation. Imagine that all your negative energy, past mistakes, distorted conceptions, and disturbing emotions leave your body with the breath in the form of dark smoke or fog. This smoke goes out into space, where it disappears completely. Don't worry that you are polluting the environment—just imagine that the smoke becomes non-existent. Feel confident that you have freed yourself of every trace of faults and negativity.

Concentrate on this experience—breathing out the dark smoke of your problems and breathing in the white light of good energy—for as long as you wish. When you are distracted by thoughts or other experiences, simply observe them without reacting or getting involved. You can also transform these distractions into dark smoke and breathe them out into oblivion.

Dedication Conclude the meditation by dedicating your positive energy to all beings finding everlasting happiness and peace of mind.

3

Meditation on Tara, the Buddha of Enlightened Activity

ara is a buddha who represents in particular all enlightened beings' skillful activities, or the means by which they communicate with and guide us according to our ability. Lama Zopa Rinpoche explained: "All actions of the Buddha manifest in the female form, Tara, to help sentient beings successfully accomplish both temporal and ultimate happiness." Because she represents action—the capacity to act, to cut through obstacles, and to be successful—she also represents courage and power. Contemplating Tara brings quick results in whatever we want and need.

The story of Tara begins long ago, when she was born as a princess named Wisdom Moon, who was very devoted to the Buddha and his followers. She generated bodhichitta, the aspiration to become a buddha herself in order to help all beings, and also made the following vow: "There are many who desire enlightenment in a man's body, but none who work for the benefit of sentient beings in the body of a woman. Therefore, until samsara is empty, I shall work for the benefit of sentient beings in a woman's body."

From then on the princess dedicated herself to attaining complete enlightenment, and when she accomplished that goal, she came to be known as Tara, "the Liberator."

Tara is also known as "The Mother of all Buddhas." Lama Yeshe explained this as follows: "This is because she is the wisdom of reality, and all buddhas and bodhisattvas are born

Green Tara

from this wisdom. This wisdom is also the fundamental cause of happiness, and of our own spiritual growth. That is why Tara is called the Mother."

She is our mother too, because she awakens—and helps fulfill—our potential to attain enlightenment.

The practice

Motivation Relax your body and still your thoughts. Think that you will do this meditation for the benefit of all living beings.

Visualize in the space before you Tara, manifestation of all that is positive. Her body is of emerald-green light, translucent and radiant. (You can visualize her any size you like.)

Her left leg is drawn up, signifying complete control over sexual energy, and her right leg is extended, indicating that she is ready to rise to the aid of all beings. Her left hand is at her heart in the refuge gesture: palm facing outward, thumb and ring finger touching, and the remaining three fingers raised.

Her right hand is on her right knee in the gesture of granting sublime realizations: palm facing outward, with the fingers loosely pointing down.

In each hand she holds the stem of a blue utpala flower, symbol of the unblocking of the central channel. She is exquisitely beautiful and smiles lovingly at you. Her clothing is of celestial silk and her ornaments of precious gems.

Concentrate for some time on the visualization, opening your heart to the energy of Tara's inexhaustible loving-kindness.

Next, think of your problems, your needs and aims, and make a prayer to Tara from your heart, asking her for help. She responds at once by sending streams of light into you: white light flows from her forehead into yours, eliminating all obstacles and negativities of body; red light flows from her throat into yours, eliminating all obstacles and negativities of speech; and blue light flows from her heart into yours, eliminating all obstacles and negativities of mind. Visualize each of these in turn; really feel that you are now completely free of all problems and that you have received the inspiration and energy to accomplish your objectives.

If you wish, you can recite Tara's mantra while doing these visualizations, and for some time afterwards: *om tare tuttare ture svaha* (pronounced *om ta-ray too-ta-ray too-ray so-ha*. For an explanation of the mantra, see page 216).

Then, Tara comes to the space above your head, facing the same way as you. She dissolves into green light, which descends through the crown of your head to your heart-center, the seat of your consciousness. Your mind merges indistinguishably with Tara's mind and you experience clarity, tranquillity, and bliss.

Remain in this state as long as possible. When thoughts arise, simply observe them with detachment, judging them as neither good nor bad, and return your attention to the experience of clarity and bliss.

Dedication At the end of the session, dedicate the positive energy you generated to all living beings, that they might attain the great joy of liberation from confusion and suffering.

(For another meditation on Tara and her mantra, see page 211.)

4

Meditation on Avalokiteshvara, the Buddha of Compassion

Whereas love is wanting others to be happy, compassion is wanting them to be free from suffering, and doing what we can to bring this about.

Compassion needs to be distinguished from pity, the sad, anxious feeling we often experience when we see or hear about people's pain. Pity is fear- and ego-based, and wants to keep a distance from the person who is suffering. Compassion, on the other hand, is based on love: it empathizes, or feels *with*, others' suffering, and is willing to get close and help them.

Compassion is also not the emotional over-involvement in others' problems that causes us to feel depressed and helpless—that is "idiot compassion." True compassion involves wisdom that understands how and why suffering occurs, and enables us to deal calmly and realistically with people and their problems. We do what we can to help, but we also understand our limitations and don't feel upset about what we cannot do.

An *attitude* of compassion is what really counts; it's not possible for anyone, even an enlightened being, to actually eliminate someone else's suffering. Each person must do that for themselves. Also, our ability to help others is limited as long as our own mind is still troubled by misconceptions and confused emotions. We should, therefore, work simultaneously on developing the wisdom to see clearly how things are and the compassionate wish to alleviate others' suffering—then our actions will be truly skillful.

Avalokiteshvara, the Buddha of Compassion

Compassion benefits not only others but ourselves as well. As the Dalai Lama has said, "If you want others to be happy, practice loving-compassion; if you want yourself to be happy, practice loving-compassion."

We all possess the potential to be limitlessly compassionate. A powerful way of awakening and developing this potential is by visualizing Avalokiteshvara (Tibetan: Chenrezig), the embodiment of compassion, and contemplating his mantra.

A mantra is a series of syllables that corresponds to certain subtle vibrations within us. Originating from enlightened minds, a mantra has built up its energy for good by being used by millions of people for thousands of years. Its effectiveness does not lie in our understanding its literal meaning but in concentrating on its sound as we recite it aloud or silently.

Avalokiteshvara's mantra, *om mani padme hum* (pronounced *om mah-nee ped-may hoom*), expresses the pure energy of compassion that exists in every being. *Om* symbolizes the enlightened state we wish to attain. *Mani* means jewel, and symbolizes compassion, love, and bodhichitta. *Padme* means lotus, which symbolizes wisdom. *Hum* indicates indivisibility. So altogether, the syllables mean that by practicing compassion and wisdom indivisibly, we can transform ourselves into enlightened beings and be of benefit to everyone.

Reciting *om mani padme hum*, either in meditation or while going about our daily activities, not only awakens our own compassion but, by joining with the millions of other people saying it too, adds to the growth of peaceful, loving energy in the world. At the very least, concentrating on the compassion-mantra helps our mind stay alert and positive rather than scattered and negative.

This practice combines an analytical meditation for generating compassion with a stabilizing meditation on the image and mantra of Avalokiteshvara.

The practice

Motivation Relax your body and mind and bring your awareness to the present by mindfully watching your breath. Check your thoughts and feelings and generate a positive motivation for doing the meditation.

Imagine that all of space is filled with beings, sitting around you and extending beyond the horizon. If you find it difficult to think of all beings, think of as many as you can, comfortably. Your parents and other family members are beside you, friends behind you, people you don't get along with in front of you, and others all around.

Contemplate the suffering of these people and beings. First, think of the suffering of your parents and the other people you are close to. Open your heart to the physical and psychological problems they are experiencing and think that, just like you, they want to be free of all suffering. Feel how wonderful it would be if they *were* free and could enjoy the peace and bliss of enlightenment.

Then think of the people you do not like or who have hurt you. Imagine their suffering: physical pain and discomfort, feelings of loneliness, insecurity, fear, dissatisfaction. Just like you, they don't want problems but they have no choice: as long as the mind is confused and ignorant of reality, it cannot find peace. Open your heart to these people for whom normally you feel irritation or anger.

Expand your awareness to take in the troubles and pain of other human beings and of animals; whoever has an uncontrolled mind necessarily has suffering.

But don't be overwhelmed by all of this! Remember that suffering, unhappiness, and pain are mental experiences, impermanent and changeable. They arise because of misunderstanding and confused emotions, and once their causes have been eliminated they disappear. It is a matter of each one of us working on our own mind, dealing with our misconceptions and negative energy and gradually developing a correct understanding of the way things actually exist.

Feel strongly the aspiration to do this yourself, so that you can help others to be free of their suffering.

Now, visualize just above your head and facing the same way as you Avalokiteshvara, the manifestation of pure unobstructed compassion, love, and wisdom. His body is of white light, transparent and radiant. Try to feel his living presence.

His face is peaceful and smiling, and he radiates his love to you and all the beings surrounding you. He has four arms. His first two hands are together at his heart and hold a jewel that fulfills all wishes; his second two are raised to the level of his shoulders, the right holding a crystal rosary and the left a white lotus. He is sitting on a white moon disk upon an open lotus, his legs crossed in the full-lotus posture. He wears exquisite silk and precious jewels.

Hold your awareness on this visualization until it is stable. Stay relaxed and comfortable and open to Avalokiteshvara's serene and loving energy.

Now, make a prayer from your heart, to overcome your misconceptions and negative energy and to develop pure love and compassion for all beings. Feel that you are connecting with your own true nature, your highest potential.

In response to your request, Avalokiteshvara lovingly sends streams of white light, filling every cell and atom of your body. It purifies all your negativities and problems, all your past harmful actions and your potential to give harm in the future, and completely fills you with his limitless love and compassion. Your body feels light and blissful, your mind peaceful and clear.

The light from Avalokiteshvara radiates out to every living being, purifying their negative energy and filling them with bliss.

Now, while concentrating on this visualization, recite the mantra, *om mani padme hum,* aloud for a while and then silently, as many times as you like.

When you have finished the recitation, visualize Avalokiteshvara dissolving into white light, which flows down through the crown of your head and reaches your heart-center. Your mind merges indistinguishably with Avalokiteshvara's mind and you experience complete tranquillity and bliss.

Hold this feeling as long as possible. Whenever your usual sense of I starts to arise—an I that is bored, restless, hungry, whatever—think that this is not your real self. Simply bring your attention back again and again to the experience of oneness with the qualities of Avalokiteshvara's mind: infinite love and compassion.

Dedication Finally, dedicate the positive energy you have created by doing this meditation to the happiness of all living beings. (For another meditation on Avalokiteshvara, see page 200.)

5

Inner Heat Meditation

This meditation is an especially powerful Vajrayana method for tapping and skillfully utilizing our innate blissful mental energy.

There is an intimate relationship between our mind and subtle nervous system. Mental energy flows through the body within a psychic nervous system composed of thousands of thin, transparent, subtle channels. The principal ones—known as the central, right, and left channels—run parallel to and just in front of the spinal column. Pure mental energy can function only within the central channel, whereas deluded energy flows through all the others.

At present, our central channel is blocked by knots of negative energy—anger, jealousy, desire, pride, and so forth—at points (*chakras*) corresponding to the base of the spine, navel, heart, throat, and crown. To the extent that this deluded energy is active, the pure energy of mind is blocked and unable to function. Recall, for example, the enormous physical and mental tension created by strong desire or anger; there is no space at all for calmness and clarity.

The inner heat meditation is an excellent method for transforming this powerful energy and developing spontaneous control over all our actions of body, speech, and mind. Mere suppression of attachment, anger, and other emotions does not eliminate them; it compounds them. The solution is literally to transform this energy—which by its nature is neither good nor bad—into blissful, free-flowing energy.

Skillful practice of the meditation will show us that we are capable of happiness and satisfaction without needing to rely upon external objects—an idea that is inconceivable for most of us.

This practice also helps us in our development of single-pointed concentration. Normally, our dissatisfied mind wanders uncontrollably, blown here and there by the force of deluded energy in the psychic channels; yet if we could have an experience of bliss pleasurable enough to concentrate on, we simply would not *want* to wander elsewhere.

The practice

Motivation Sit comfortably in your meditation place and generate a strong positive motivation for doing this inner heat practice. Determine to keep your mind relaxed, concentrated, and free of expectations for the entire session.

Start by visualizing the central channel as a transparent, hollow tube, a finger's breadth in diameter. It runs straight down through the center of the body, just in front of the spinal column, from the crown of your head to the base of your spine.

Next, visualize the right and left lateral channels, slightly thinner than the central one. They start from the right and left nostrils respectively, travel upward to the top of the head and then curve over to run downward on either side of the central channel. They curve inward and join the central channel at a point approximately four fingers' breadth below the level of the navel.

Take as long as you like to construct this visualization. Once it is stable, imagine a red-hot ember the size of a tiny seed inside the central channel at the level of the navel. To strengthen this visualization, imagine reaching into a fire, taking out a tiny glowing ember and placing it in your central channel. Once it is there, really feel its intense heat.

Now, in order to increase the heat, gently contract the muscles of the pelvic floor, concentrating on the internal rather than the external muscles, and in this way bring air energy up from the lowest chakra to the ember.

Next, gently take a full breath through both nostrils. The air travels from the nostrils down through the right and left channels to where they enter the central channel just below the level of the navel. The air joins with the heat there and with the energy brought up from below.

As you stop inhaling, immediately swallow and push down gently with your diaphragm in order to firmly compress the energy brought down from above: now the air energy is completely locked in, compressed from above and below.

Now, hold your breath as long as it is comfortable to do so. Concentrate completely on the ember in the navel area, whose heat is increasing and spreading as a result of the compressed air energy.

When you are ready, relax your lightly tensed muscles and exhale gently and completely. Although the air leaves through the nostrils, visualize that it rises up through the central channel and dissolves there. The heat emanating from the burning ember at the navel continually increases and spreads and starts to burn away the blockages at each chakra and to warm the concentration of silvery blissful energy found at the crown chakra.

However, the focal point of your concentration is always the heat of the burning ember in the navel area.

Once your first exhalation is complete, again tighten the lower muscles, inhale a second time, swallow and push down with the diaphragm, thus again compressing the air and intensifying the heat. Hold your breath and concentrate on the heat, then exhale, releasing the air up the central channel once again.

Repeat the entire cycle rhythmically seven times altogether, the intensity of the heat growing with every breath.

At the seventh exhalation, imagine that the now burning hot ember explodes into flames. They shoot up the central channel, completely consuming and purifying the deluded energy at each chakra. At the crown, the flames finally melt and release the silvery blissful energy, which pours down the purified central channel giving increasing pleasure at each chakra it passes. Finally, when it meets the blazing ember at the navel chakra, there is an explosion of bliss. This blissful heat flows out to every atom and cell of your body, completely filling you, making your mind very happy.

Concentrate on this pleasure without tension or expectation; without clinging to it or analyzing it. Just relax and enjoy it.

You will notice that, no matter how strong the pleasure is, your mind and body are calm and controlled, unlike our usual experiences of physical pleasure when the mind is excited and uncontrolled.

If your mind should wander from its concentration to other objects—the past or future, objects of attachment or aversion—focus your attention on the *subject* of the thought, the mind that perceives the distracting object, the thinker. Watch the subject until the distracting thought disappears, then concentrate again on the blissful feeling.

Analysis of feeling: Having reached a state of clarity, it is good to use it to discover the nature of your mind. After concentrating on your feeling, being absorbed in it for some time, analyze it by contemplating each of the following questions. Take as long as you like.

> Is the feeling permanent or impermanent? How? Why?
> Is the feeling blissful or suffering? How? Why?
> Is the feeling related or unrelated to the nervous system
>   and the mind? How? Why?
> Does the feeling exist inherently, from its own side,
>   without depending on anything else, or not? How?
>   Why?
> Examine each point from every angle.

Dedication Finish the session by summing up your conclusion, then dedicate any positive energy and insight gained during the meditation to your speedy enlightenment for the sake of all living beings.

Part Six

PRAYERS AND OTHER DEVOTIONAL PRACTICES

About Devotion

Faith

The idea of devotion makes some people uneasy because they equate it with blind faith and mindless submissiveness. But proper devotion is not like that. It is, in fact, a very positive attitude: to be devoted to one's family, friends, or work is to have love, care, and responsibility. In this sense it means going beyond our usual narrow, self-centered thoughts and concerns, and dedicating our energy to others.

In a religious or spiritual sense, devotion involves faith. In Buddhism faith is a positive mental state, and is explained as clarity, conviction, and aspiration with regard to someone or something that exists (as opposed to something imaginary) and has excellent qualities and abilities. There are three kinds of faith: one is recognizing and appreciating the good qualities of a person or object, another is aspiring to emulate those qualities, and the third is conviction based on having studied and contemplated the teaching given by someone such as the Buddha. This third kind of faith is the best as it is rational and stable, and it is said to be the source of all happiness and goodness.

Of course, if our faith and devotion are not well-founded or their object is unreliable, we will only be disappointed and feel doubt and resentment. But if it is based on clear, correct understanding and its object is one that will not let us down, the experience will be rich and productive.

Refuge

In Buddhism, devotion is associated with refuge, the first step on the path to liberation and awakening. Refuge is the attitude of relying upon, or turning to, something for guidance and help. In an ordinary sense we take refuge in friends for love and security, in food and entertainment when we are hungry and bored, and so forth. But such external sources of refuge can satisfy our needs only temporarily because they, as well as the happiness they bring, are impermanent and unreliable.

Buddhist refuge, on the other hand, involves discovering and utilizing the unlimited potential that lies within each of us. There are two aspects of refuge, outer and inner. Outer refuge is appreciating and relying upon the Three Jewels: Buddha, Dharma, and Sangha.

Buddha refers both to the enlightened state itself—the removal of all negative qualities and the perfection of all positive—and to those who have attained enlightenment. Refuge in Buddha means opening our heart to the love and wisdom offered by these beings and accepting their guidance on the spiritual path.

Dharma refers to wisdom, the realizations that comprise the progressive stages of the path to enlightenment. The literal meaning of the Sanskrit term *Dharma* is "to hold"—it includes any method that holds or protects us from problems. Buddha's teachings are known as Dharma because they come from his actual experience of eliminating every trace of confusion and negative energy from his mind. Refuge in Dharma means practicing the prescribed methods, aspiring to awaken within ourselves the wisdom that every enlightened being has discovered.

Sangha refers to the spiritual community, those who have wisdom and give us inspiration and support. Buddha and Dharma provide us with the basis of our practice but Sangha provide the help we need to make the practice actually work. Talking with like-minded friends, for example, can give us answers to questions and solutions to problems; meditating together gives us strength and encouragement; a community of meditators offers a peaceful haven from the craziness of city life. Refuge in Sangha means respecting such friends and accepting their help.

Inner refuge is refuge in ourselves, in our ultimate potential. The three refuge objects have their internal counterparts: the inner buddha is the seed of enlightenment that lies in the mind of every sentient being, without exception; the inner dharma is our natural wisdom that can distinguish real from false; the inner sangha is the guidance and inspiration that we can give others. As human beings, we have the potential to develop unlimited love, compassion, and wisdom and to free ourselves from all negative energy—in other words, to reach the same level as a buddha.

Usually we find it difficult to feel good about ourselves and to have confidence in our own potential—instead we take refuge in outside things. Just imagine the boredom, the uneasiness, and the games the mind would play if we were completely alone for a day, or even an hour, cut off from people, books, television and all external means of occupying ourselves! We can't conceive of living without sense objects—the external world. However, it *is* possible to be completely satisfied and happy, whatever the situation, by relying solely on our inner resources. The external refuge objects exist to awaken us to these resources, to our inner buddha, dharma, and sangha. When we recognize and nourish this potential, we have found the real meaning of refuge.

Refuge is a fundamental step on the spiritual path, and devotion is an essential component of it. It should not be an ignorant, emotional attitude, but one that is sound and intelligent, based on clear understanding of what Buddha, Dharma, and Sangha really are and what they can do for us. We *do* need help to travel the path to inner awakening, but we need to check carefully the qualifications of the teachers we meet and the effectiveness of their methods, not just follow the advice of anyone with a nice vibration or a charismatic personality. It's a question of getting to know a teacher or a path, examining, reflecting, experimenting, being honest and sincere. All this may take some time, but it is very important to make sure that any devotion we do cultivate will be appropriate and productive, not a waste of energy.

If you don't feel such faith, you can simply read through this section, or experiment with the methods if you like.

The purpose and psychological effects of the practices are explained here as clearly as possible, but the real taste comes only by doing them, with understanding and devotion.

1

Prayers

The success of any project—climbing a mountain, writing a book, or baking a cake—hinges on the care we take in the preparatory work. The same is true for meditation. A successful meditation session depends primarily on our state of mind, and the appropriate inner state can be induced through reciting certain prayers, verbally or mentally, with understanding and sincerity.

Prayer is not the mechanical repetition of words but an opening of the heart to communicate with our true nature. The words serve as a reminder of what we are trying to achieve, and actually help create the cause for whatever we re praying for to occur in the future.

Prayers to be said at the start of a meditation session

1. Prayer of refuge and bodhichitta

> I go for refuge until I am enlightened
> To the Buddha, the Dharma, and the Supreme
>   Assembly.
> By my practice of giving and other perfections,
> May I become a Buddha to benefit all sentient beings.
>   (3 times)

2. The four immeasurable thoughts

> May all sentient beings have happiness and the causes
>   of happiness;

May all sentient beings be free from suffering and the
   causes of suffering;
May all sentient beings be inseparable from the
   happiness that is free from suffering;
May all sentient beings abide in equanimity, free from
   attachment and anger that hold some close and others
   distant.

3. Refuge in the guru

The guru is Buddha, the guru is Dharma,
The guru is Sangha, also;
The guru is the creator of all (happiness);
To all gurus I go for refuge. (3 times)

4. The seven limbs

Reverently, I prostrate with my body, speech and mind;
I present clouds of every type of offering, actual and
   imagined;
I declare all my negative actions accumulated since
   beginningless time
And rejoice in the merit of all holy and ordinary beings.
Please, remain until the end of cyclic existence
And turn the wheel of Dharma for living beings.
I dedicate my own merits and those of all others to the
   great enlightenment.

5. Mandala offering

Om vajra ground *ah hum*.
Mighty golden ground.
Om vajra fence *ah hum*.
Outside it is encircled by the surrounding wall,
In the center of which are Sumeru, King of
   Mountains;
The eastern continent Videha,
The southern, Jambudvipa,
The western, Godaniya,

The northern, Kuru,

[The eastern minor continents] Deha and Videha, [the
southern] Chamara and Aparachamara, [the western]
Satha and Uttaramantrin, [and the northern] Kuru
and Kaurava.

[In the four continents are:] [East] the precious
mountain, [South] the wish-granting tree, [West] the
wish-fulfilling cow, [North] the unploughed harvest.

[On the first level are:]
the precious wheel, the precious jewel,
the precious queen, the precious minister,
the precious elephant, the precious horse,
the precious general, and the great treasure vase.

[On the second level, the eight goddesses:] Lady of
grace, lady of garlands, lady of song, lady of dance,
lady of flowers, lady of incense, lady of lamps,
lady of perfume.

[On the third level:] The sun and the moon; the precious
parasol; and the banner of victory in all quarters.

In the center, the most perfect riches of gods and human
beings, with nothing missing, pure and delightful.

To my glorious, holy and most kind root and lineage
gurus, and in particular to the deity host of Lama
Tsongkhapa, King of Sages, Maha-Vajradhara, and
their divine retinue, I shall offer these as a
buddhafield.

Please accept them with compassion for the sake of
migrating beings.

Having accepted them, to me and all migrating mother
sentient beings as far as the limits of space, out of your
great compassion, please grant your inspiration!

Short outer mandala

This ground, anointed with perfume, strewn with flowers,
Adorned with Mount Meru, four continents, the sun and
the moon:

I imagine this as a buddhafield and offer it.
May all living beings enjoy this pure land!

Inner mandala

The objects of my attachment, aversion, and ignorance—
    friends, enemies, and strangers—
And my body, wealth, and enjoyments;
Without any sense of loss, I offer this collection.
Please accept it with pleasure
And bless me with freedom from the three poisons.

Idam guru ratna mandalakam niryatayami
(I send forth this jeweled mandala to you, precious gurus.)

Prayers to be said at the conclusion of a meditation session

6. Dedication of merit

Due to the merits of these virtuous actions
May I quickly attain the state of a guru-buddha
And lead all living beings, without exception,
Into that enlightened state.

7. Bodhichitta prayer

May the supreme jewel bodhichitta
That has not arisen, arise and grow;
And may that which has arisen not diminish
But increase more and more.

2

Explanation of the Prayers

1. Prayer of refuge and bodhichitta

This prayer expresses the most positive, beneficial intention we could have for engaging in study or meditation on the path to enlightenment.

The first part of the prayer deals with *refuge,* the attitude of turning to the Buddha, Dharma, and Sangha (the latter being also called the "Supreme Assembly") for guidance and help (see page 168). Remember the two aspects of refuge, outer and inner, and feel confident that the seed of enlightenment lies within your own mind.

The second part of the prayer is the generation of *bodhichitta,* the mind set on enlightenment. Bodhichitta, founded on pure love and compassion for every living being, is the dedicated determination to become a buddha solely to help others achieve enlightenment too.

The path of an enlightenment-bound person—a bodhisattva—involves the development of the *six perfections* (Sanskrit: *paramita*): giving, moral discipline, patience, joyous effort, concentration, and wisdom. These six, practiced with the motive of helping others achieve enlightenment, provide nourishment for the seed of enlightenment to grow in our own mind. The gradual development of each perfection progressively erodes our delusions, making space for the wisdom that understands reality.

Anything we do—meditation, eating, sleeping, or working, automatically becomes a cause for enlightenment if it is done with the thought of bodhichitta.

Refuge and bodhichitta give life and meaning to our meditations. You can recite the prayer three times before every session,
and it is best if you can also visualize the Buddha in front of you
(see page 186), seeing him as the embodiment of the qualities you
are trying to develop within yourself.

2. The four immeasurable thoughts

The four thoughts expressed in this prayer are called immeasurable because they extend to all beings throughout the infinite
universe. The first is *immeasurable love:* the wish for all beings to
be happy. The second is *immeasurable compassion:* the wish for all
beings to be free of suffering. The third is *immeasurable joy:* the
wish for all beings to experience the ultimate happiness that lasts
forever. The fourth is *immeasurable equanimity:* the wish for all
beings to be free of the attachment and aversion that cause us to
distinguish between friend, enemy, and stranger.

Each line of the prayer is a meditation in itself and its heartfelt
recitation creates the cause for our development of universal
awareness and concern for others.

3. Refuge in the guru

There are countless beings who have reached enlightenment,
and these buddhas actively help all sentient beings. The most
effective way they help is by instructing us in the knowledge and
techniques of the path to enlightenment. Because of our obscurations we are unable to perceive enlightened beings directly, so
they reach us through spiritual teachers (Sanskrit: *guru;* Tibetan:
lama). By recognizing our teachers as one with the buddhas, we
are able to make direct contact with the enlightened state and
eventually to actualize it ourselves. This practice, known as
guru-yoga, is the essential method for realizing the entire path
to enlightenment.

In this prayer we identify the guru with the three objects of
refuge, recognizing that without the guru there would be no
Buddha, Dharma, or Sangha and, consequently, no true happiness.

4. The seven limbs

Manjushri, the buddha of wisdom, once gave advice to Je Tsong-khapa on how to attain realizations. He said three things should be practiced together: (1) praying sincerely to the guru, seeing him or her as one with the buddha; (2) purifying the mind of negative imprints and accumulating merit, that is, positive energy and insights; and (3) meditating upon the subjects one wants to realize. Cultivating these three creates the correct causes and conditions for actualizing in our minds the various stages of the path to enlightenment.

The second—purifying negative imprints and accumulating positive energy and insight—is most successfully achieved by the practice of the seven limbs. As the body needs its four limbs to be a whole body, so too does any meditation practice need its seven limbs in order to be complete.

Each limb can be practiced extensively; they are encapsulated, however, in the prayer of the seven limbs.

i. *Prostration:* Prostrating is a means of showing appreciation and respect for the Buddha, Dharma, and Sangha, and is a powerful way to purify negativities, especially pride, which directly prevents our growth of wisdom. There are three ways of making prostrations: physical, verbal, and mental.

Physical prostrations can be performed in various ways. The most common method among Tibetan Buddhists is as follows. Begin in a standing position, touch your joined hands to the crown of your head, forehead, throat, and heart, then fall to your hands and knees, touch your forehead to the floor and rise.

To do a full-length prostration—more effective in purifying negative energy—touch your joined hands to the crown of your head, forehead, throat, and heart, fall to your hands and knees, then stretch your entire body on the floor, face down, with your arms straight out in front of you. (It would be best to have someone demonstrate these for you, so you can see the correct way to do them.)

Verbal prostration is expressing the good qualities of the refuge objects.

Mental prostration is the respect, faith, and confidence in the three objects of refuge that accompany physical and verbal prostration. This mental attitude is the essence of the practice and its depth and sincerity determine the power of prostrations.

ii. *Offering:* We delight in giving gifts to friends and sharing pleasant experiences with them. In a spiritual sense we offer beautiful objects, positive thoughts and actions, and the pure experience of bliss to our objects of refuge. Making offerings is a powerful antidote to selfishness and attachment and a principal means of accumulating the positive energy crucial to our development of wisdom.

Actual offerings, mentioned in the prayer, are those physically offered (on an altar, for example) to the objects of refuge, while *imagined offerings* are those we visualize. The essence of any action, and what determines its worth, is the state of one's mind at the time it is done. Simple, insignificant objects can be visualized and offered as the most beautiful sights, sounds, tastes, smells, and tangible things imaginable; the benefit of such an offering is enormous.

It is said that a young boy who reverently offered a handful of sand to the Buddha, visualizing it as gold, was later reborn as the great Indian King Ashoka, largely as a result of the merit of this offering.

Imagined offerings can be made at any time: whatever beautiful and pleasing object we encounter can be offered in our heart to the objects of refuge, and the merit of the offering dedicated to our attainment of enlightenment for the benefit of all beings. In this way we can be accumulating the causes of enlightenment continually while going about our daily life.

iii. *Confession:* As discussed in the meditation on karma (page 80), actions of body, speech, and mind that are motivated by delusion—attachment, aversion, confusion, jealousy, pride, and the like—are negative, or unskillful, actions because they result in future misfortune and cause us to remain in cyclic existence. However, they can be rectified, and their resultant imprints on the mind purified, through the practice of confession.

There are four steps in this largely internal practice—the four opponent powers—and the success of our purification is measured by the strength and sincerity of our practice of these four. (See further discussion of these four in the purification practices on pages 90 and 219.)

The power of regret. This is the attitude of first acknowledging and then regretting our negative or unskillful actions, because we understand that they will cause suffering to ourselves and others in the future. Regret is not like guilt, which involves negative fear and anxiety; rather, it is an intelligent and honest recognition of the nature of our actions and their results.

The power of reliance. When we fall on the ground it hurts us, but we also need to rely on the ground to get back up. Similarly, since we create most negative actions in relation either to the Three Jewels or other sentient beings, we rely on these objects to avert the suffering which results from such actions. Hence the power of reliance is taking refuge in Buddha, Dharma, and Sangha and regenerating our bodhichitta. For those who are not Buddhist, this power can involve renewing your commitment to whatever objects of devotion or spiritual goals you hold in your heart, and generating the wish to help and not harm others.

The power of remedy. The third step in the process of purification is the practice of positive actions such as offering, prostration, mantra recitation, and meditation, especially on emptiness, which counteract the force of previous negative actions.

The power of resolve. The final step is the firm determination to avoid doing the same negative actions again. Of course, some actions are easier to avoid than others; it might be realistic to promise never to kill again, but it would be unrealistic to promise never to lose our temper again, for example. In cases like this it would be practical to promise not to do the action for an hour or a day, then gradually extend the period of time as we learn to gain more control over our mind.

Determination is crucial to our success in any venture, especially in our efforts to subdue the mind.

iv. *Rejoicing:* Rejoicing in the well-being of others is a powerful antidote to jealousy and resentment—frequent responses when someone else succeeds or is happy. Jealousy is a tense, unhappy state of mind that cannot bear the happiness of others; rejoicing is light and open, a loving response that allows us to share in their happiness. The benefit, then, is immediate, and we also create the cause to experience happiness ourselves in the future.

We rejoice also in the *causes* of happiness: the positive actions of all beings, holy and ordinary; and wish that they will continue to be created as much as possible. We can rejoice at any time, in any place—we don't need to be sitting in meditation. It is one of the easiest, and most necessary, methods of transforming our mind.

v. *Requesting the buddhas not to pass away:* Although the buddhas always exist and work continuously to help sentient beings, we can connect with them only if we create the appropriate causes. Requesting them to remain in the world and guide us is primarily for our own benefit: it purifies our mind of negative actions done in the past in relation to gurus and buddhas and helps us to open our mind and truly appreciate their help and inspiration. Requesting the buddhas to stay also creates the cause for our own long life.

vi. *Requesting the buddhas to turn the wheel of Dharma:* Requesting the buddhas to teach the way to enlightenment enhances our appreciation of the Dharma and counteracts past attitudes of disrespect toward spiritual teachings. Especially, it lays the foundation for never being separated from teachers who can guide us spiritually and for always having the teachings available.

vii. *Dedication:* It is very important at the beginning of any meditation or other positive action to have a clear understanding of our motivation; it is equally important to conclude the action by dedicating the merit—the good energy and insight—we have created by doing it. We do this by recalling our initial motivating thought, renewing our aspiration to reach a certain goal, and sending our merit in that direction. Motivation and dedication ensure that our positive energy is not lost and that the results will come. Otherwise, there is no firm imprint put onto the mind, and any good done can easily be destroyed by anger or other negative actions.

The best dedication is to pray that the meditation or action we have just done will become a cause for our enlightenment for the sake of all sentient beings.

5. Mandala offering

The mandala offering involves mentally transforming the entire universe—everything that exists—into a pure realm and offering it to the objects of refuge. The main purpose of doing this practice is to accumulate merit, which is needed in the cultivation of insight and wisdom.

Seeds for our growth on the path to enlightenment are planted in our mind through hearing or reading the teachings. These seeds need the nourishment of merit—strong, positive energy—in order to grow and produce insights and realizations. Offering the mandala is said to be one of the best means of providing this nourishment. It also has immediate benefits: giving from the heart in this way is a remedy for attachment and miserliness.

The prayer is written in terms of Buddhist cosmology, in which Mount Meru is a jeweled mountain in the center of the universe and the four continents are different realms of human life. The mandala you offer can accord with either Eastern or Western cosmology, whichever you feel most comfortable with, but the point is to offer *everything*—all the various worlds and realms of living beings and all the beautiful things we enjoy.

Visualize a miniature version of the entire universe in the space in front of you and then transform it into a pure realm. The environment and beings of a pure realm are completely, perfectly beautiful and make the mind peaceful and happy; use your imagination to create a blissful paradise.

Impure objects give rise to attachment, irritation, and confusion, while pure objects give rise to clear, positive states of mind, especially the wisdom understanding reality and the experience of great bliss.

Offer this pure land to the refuge objects, without clinging to any part of it, and feel that your gift is accepted with love and the highest appreciation.

The *inner mandala* adds another dimension. Here you bring to mind the people and things—including your body and belongings—for which you have attachment, aversion, and indifference. Visualize these objects, transformed into pure objects in the mandala, and offer them all to the buddhas. Having completely given them up, there is now no need to have attachment, dislike, or ignorance—the three poisons—toward any person or thing.

6. Dedication of merit and

7. The bodhichitta prayer

See the explanation of *dedication* under *The seven limbs* on page 177.

At the conclusion of a session of meditation or instruction, the merit generated during the session should be directed to a worthwhile goal—in this case, enlightenment. Reciting these two verses reminds us of the bodhichitta motivation: the aspiration to develop love and compassion for all beings and to attain enlightenment in order to help them. Our merit is thus dedicated to the welfare of others; this is the best dedication we could make.

3
A Short Meditation on the Graduated Path to Enlightenment

This prayer, composed by Je Tsongkhapa, summarizes the stages of the graduated path to enlightenment as taught by Shakyamuni Buddha and elucidated by Atisha, the eleventh-century Indian pandit.

The foundation of all good qualities is the kind and
    venerable guru;
Correct devotion to him is the root of the path.
By clearly seeing this and applying great effort,
Please bless me to rely upon him with great respect.

Understanding that the precious freedom of this rebirth
    is found only once,
Is greatly meaningful, and is difficult to find again,
Please bless me to generate the mind that unceasingly,
Day and night, takes its essence.

This life is as impermanent as a water bubble;
Remember how quickly it decays and death comes.
After death, just like a shadow follows the body,
The results of black and white karma follow.
Finding firm and definite conviction in this,
Please bless me always to be careful
To abandon even the slightest negativities
And accomplish all virtuous deeds.

Seeking samsaric pleasures is the door to all suffering:
They are uncertain and cannot be relied upon.
Recognizing these shortcomings,
Please bless me to generate the strong wish for the bliss
    of liberation.

Led by this pure thought,
Mindfulness, alertness and great caution arise.
The root of the teachings is keeping the pratimoksha
    vows:
Please bless me to accomplish this essential practice.

Just as I have fallen into the sea of samsara,
So have all mother migratory beings.
Please bless me to see this, train in supreme bodhichitta,
And bear the responsibility of freeing migratory beings.

Even if I develop only bodhichitta, but I don't practice
    the three types of morality,
I will not achieve enlightenment.
With my clear recognition of this,
Please bless me to practice the bodhisattva vows with
    great energy.

Once I have pacified distractions to wrong objects
And correctly analyzed the meaning of reality,
Please bless me to generate quickly within my
    mindstream
The unified path of calm abiding and special insight.

Having become a pure vessel by training in the
    general path,
Please bless me to enter
The holy gateway of the fortunate ones:
The supreme vajra vehicle.

At that time, the basis of accomplishing the two
    attainments
Is keeping pure vows and samaya.
As I have become firmly convinced of this,
Please bless me to protect these vows and pledges like
    my life.

Then, having realized the importance of the two stages,
The essence of the Vajrayana,
By practicing with great energy, never giving up the
    four sessions,
Please bless me to realize the teachings of the holy guru.

Like that, may the gurus who show the noble path
And the spiritual friends who practice it have long lives.
Please bless me to pacify completely
All outer and inner hindrances.

In all my lives, never separated from perfect gurus,
May I enjoy the magnificent Dharma.
By completing the qualities of the stages and paths,
May I quickly attain the state of Vajradhara.

4

Meditation on the Buddha

uddha is a Sanskrit word that means "fully awakened." It refers not only to Shakyamuni, or Gautama, the founder of the teachings that came to be known as Buddhism, but also to any person who attains enlightenment. There are numberless enlightened beings—beings who have completely transformed their minds, eliminated all negative energy, and become whole, perfect. They are not confined to a transient, physical body as we are, but are free from death and rebirth. They can abide in a state of pure consciousness, or appear in different forms—a sunset, music, a beggar, a teacher—in order to communicate their wisdom and love to ordinary beings. They are the very essence of compassion and wisdom, and their energy is all around us, all the time.

Every living being, by virtue of having a mind, is able to become a buddha. The fundamental nature of the mind is pure, clear, and free of the clouds of disturbing conceptions and emotions that now obscure it. As long as we identify with confused states of mind, believing, "I am an angry person; I am depressed; I have so many problems," we don't even give ourselves the chance to change.

Of course, our problems *are* very deep and complex, but they are not as real or as solid as we think. We also have the wisdom that can recognize our mistaken thinking, and the capacity to give and to love. It is a matter of identifying with and gradually developing *these* qualities to the point where they arise spontaneously and effortlessly. It is not easy to become enlightened, but it is possible. In this meditation, we visualize the form of Shakyamuni Buddha and recite his mantra.

Shakyamuni was born a prince, Siddhartha, into a vastly wealthy family two-and-a-half thousand years ago in the north of India. He lived in his kingdom for twenty-nine years, sheltered from the more unpleasant realities of human existence. He eventually encountered them, however, in the form of a sick person, an old, senile person, and a corpse. These experiences affected him profoundly. His next significant encounter was with a wandering meditator who had transcended the concerns of ordinary life and reached a state of balance and serenity.

Realizing that his way of life led only to death and had no real, lasting value, Prince Siddhartha decided to leave his home and family and go to the forest to meditate. After many years of persistent, single-minded effort, meeting and overcoming one difficulty after another, he attained enlightenment—that is, he became a buddha. Having thus freed himself from all delusions and suffering, he aspired to help others reach enlightenment too; his compassion was limitless.

He was now thirty-five years old. He spent the remaining forty-five years of his life explaining the way to understand the mind, deal with problems, develop love and compassion, and thus become enlightened. His teachings were remarkably fluid, varying according to the needs, capabilities, and personalities of his listeners. He led them skillfully toward understanding the ultimate nature of reality.

The Buddha's life itself was a teaching, an example of the path to enlightenment, and his death a teaching on impermanence.

A powerful way to discover our own buddha-nature is to open ourselves to the external buddha. With continual practice, our ordinary self-image gradually falls away and we learn instead to identify with our innate wisdom and compassion: our own buddhahood.

The practice

Refuge and motivation Calm your mind by doing a few moments of meditation on the breath. Then, contemplate the prayer of taking refuge and generating a bodhichitta motivation:

Shakyamuni Buddha

> I go for refuge until I am enlightened
> To the Buddha, the Dharma, and the Supreme Assembly.
> By my practice of giving and other perfections,
> May I become a Buddha to benefit all sentient beings.
>   (3 times)

Generate love and compassion by reflecting briefly on the predicament of all beings: their wish to experience true happiness and their inability to obtain it, and their wish to avoid suffering and their continual encounters with it.

Then think: "In order to help all beings and lead them to the perfect peace and happiness of enlightenment I myself must attain enlightenment. For this purpose I shall practice this meditation."

Visualization of the Buddha Every aspect of the visualization is made of light: transparent, intangible, and radiant. At the level of your forehead and between six and eight feet away is a large golden throne adorned with jewels and supported at each of its four corners by a pair of snow lions. These animals, in reality manifestations of bodhisattvas, have white fur and a green mane and tail.

On the flat surface of the throne is a seat consisting of a large open lotus and two radiant discs representing the sun and the moon, one on top of the other. These three objects symbolize the three principal realizations of the path to enlightenment: the lotus, renunciation; the sun, emptiness; and the moon, bodhichitta.

Seated upon this is the Buddha, who has attained these realizations and is the embodiment of all enlightened beings. His body is of golden light and he wears the saffron robes of a monk. His robes do not actually touch his body but are separated from it by about an inch. He is seated in the vajra, or full-lotus, posture. The palm of his right hand rests on his right knee, the fingers touching the moon cushion, signifying his great control. His left hand rests in his lap in the meditation pose, holding a bowl filled with nectar, which is medicine for curing our disturbing states of mind and other hindrances.

Buddha's face is very beautiful. His smiling, compassionate gaze is directed at you and, simultaneously, toward every other living being. Feel that he is free of all judging, critical thoughts and that he accepts you just as you are. His eyes are long and narrow. His lips are cherry red and the lobes of his ears are long. His hair is blue-black and each hair is individually curled to the right and not mixed with the others. Every feature of his appearance represents an attribute of his omniscient mind.

Rays of light emanate from every pore of Buddha's pure body and reach every corner of the universe. These rays are actually composed of countless miniature buddhas, some going out to help living beings, others dissolving back into his body, having finished their work.

Purification Feel the living presence of Buddha and take refuge in him, recalling his perfect qualities and his willingness and ability to help you. Make a request from your heart to receive his blessings to help you to become free from all your negative energy, misconceptions, and other problems; and to receive all the realizations of the path to enlightenment.

Your request is accepted. A stream of purifying white light, which is in the nature of the enlightened mind, flows from Buddha's heart and enters your body through the crown of your head. Just as the darkness in a room is instantly dispelled the moment a light is switched on, so too is the darkness of your negative energy dispelled upon contact with this radiant white light.

As it flows into you, filling your body completely, recite the following prayer three times.

> To the guru, founder,
> Bhagavan, tathagata, arhat,
> Perfectly completed buddha,
> Glorious conqueror Shakyamuni Buddha,
> I prostrate, make offerings, and go for refuge.
> Please grant me your blessings.

Now, recite Buddha's mantra, *tadyatha om muni muni maha muniye svaha* (pronounced *ta-ya-ta om moo-nee moo-nee ma-ha moo-na-yay so-ha*). Repeat it out loud, or chant it, at least seven times, then say it quietly to yourself for a few minutes.

When you have finished reciting, feel that all your negative energy, problems and subtle obscurations have been completely purified. Your body feels blissful and light. Concentrate on this for a while.

Receiving inspiring strength Visualize that a stream of golden light descends from the Buddha's heart and flows into your body through the crown of your head. The essence of this light is the excellent qualities of his pure body, speech, and mind.

He can transform his body into different forms, animate and inanimate, to help living beings according to their individual needs and particular states of mind.

With his speech he can communicate different aspects of the Dharma simultaneously to beings of various levels of development and be understood by them in their respective languages.

His omniscient mind sees clearly every atom of existence and every occurrence—past, present, and future—and knows the thoughts of every living being: such is his awareness in every moment.

These infinite good qualities flow into every part of your body. Concentrate on this blissful experience while again repeating the mantra, *tadyatha om muni muni maha muniye svaha.*

When you have finished the recitation feel that you have received the infinite excellent qualities of Buddha's body, speech, and mind. Your body feels light and blissful. Concentrate on this for some time.

Absorption of the visualization Now, visualize that the eight snow lions absorb into the throne, the throne into the lotus and the lotus into the sun and moon. They, in turn, absorb into the Buddha, who now comes to the space above your head, melts into light, and dissolves into your body.

Your ordinary sense of I—unworthy and burdened with faults—and all your other wrong conceptions disappear completely. In that instant you become one with the Buddha's blissful, omniscient mind in the aspect of vast empty space.

Concentrate on this experience for as long as possible, allowing no other thoughts to distract you.

Enlightening all sentient beings Then, imagine that from this empty state there appear in the place where you are sitting the throne, lotus, sun, and moon, and upon these yourself as the Buddha. Everything is of the nature of light, exactly as you had visualized before in front of you. Feel that you *are* Buddha. Identify with his enlightened wisdom and compassion instead of with your usual incorrect self-view.

Surrounding you in every direction and filling all of space are all living beings. Generate love and compassion for them by recalling that they too want to achieve happiness and peace of mind and freedom from all problems. Now that you are enlightened you can help them.

At your heart are a lotus and a moon. Standing upright around the circumference of the moon, reading clockwise, are the syllables of the mantra, *tadyatha om muni muni maha muniye svaha.* The seed-syllable *mum* (pronounced *moom*) stands at the moon's center.

Visualize that rays of light—actually your wisdom and compassion—emanate from every letter and spread in all directions. They reach the countless sentient beings surrounding you and completely purify them of their obscurations and delusions and fill them with inspiration and strength.

While imagining this, again recite the mantra, *tadyatha om muni muni maha muniye svaha.*

When you have finished reciting, think: "Now I have led all sentient beings to enlightenment, thus fulfilling my intention for doing this meditation."

Visualize that everyone surrounding you is now in the form of Buddha and is experiencing complete bliss and the wisdom of emptiness.

You should not worry that your meditation is a sham and that you have not helped even one person achieve enlightenment. This practice is known as "bringing the future result into the present path" and is a powerful cause for our own enlightenment. It helps us develop firm conviction in our innate perfection—our buddha-potential; that what we have just done in meditation we will definitely accomplish one day.

Dedication Conclude the session by dedicating all the positive energy and insight you have gained by doing this meditation to your eventual attainment of enlightenment for the benefit of all living beings.

Explanation of the mantra

Tadyatha Thus

Om The enlightened state; the positive qualities of the buddhas' bodies, speech, and minds.

Muni Control—over unfortunate rebirths and self-grasping ignorance.

Muni Control—over the sufferings of cyclic existence and the self-cherishing attitude.

Maha muniye Great control—over the sufferings of subtle illusions and dualistic thinking.

Svaha May my mind receive, absorb, and keep the blessings of the mantra, and may they take root in my mind.

5

Meditation on the Healing Buddha

B uddhism places a great deal of emphasis on the interre-
lationship between our mind, our body, and our health.
Buddha explained that negative aspects of the mind lead
to sickness and unhappiness, whereas positive aspects of the
mind lead to good health and happiness. According to the Tibetan
medical system, based on teachings of the Buddha, the three "poisonous" states of mind—attachment, anger and ignorance—are at
the root of all disease.

In recent times, Western doctors and scientists have confirmed
this. Studies show that people suffering from chronic emotional
stress such as anxiety, depression, or anger and hostility have
double the average risk of becoming seriously ill. Also, many doctors and psychologists find that the source of cancer lies in negative
attitudes and that it can be cured by generating positive attitudes.

Buddhism offers a number of spiritual methods that can be
utilized in conjunction with medicine and other treatments to
overcome illness. These include living ethically, meditation practice to reduce stress, and working on disturbing emotions such as
anger, fear, and depression. There are also a number of healing
practices that involve visualizing Buddha-images and reciting
their mantras. One of the most well-known and effective of these
practices is that of the Healing Buddha, usually referred to as the
Medicine Buddha.

While on the path to enlightenment, the Medicine Buddha made
a series of vows to help sentient beings during difficult times such
as our own, when there is an increase in delusions, social problems,

Medicine Buddha

wars, natural disasters, and mental and physical diseases. The practice of Medicine Buddha is particularly beneficial for people who are ill, in a coma, or dying. But the practice is also effective in clearing away obstacles, and thus can lead to success in whatever endeavors we engage in, spiritual or ordinary.

This practice can be done for yourself, or for another person who is ill or in need of help, in which case you would visualize the Medicine Buddha above that person's head.

The practice

Sit comfortably with your back straight. Take a few minutes to settle your mind into the present moment by focusing on your breathing, and letting go of all other thoughts....

Motivation Then generate a positive motivation for doing the practice. Lama Zopa Rinpoche says that healing practice is most effective when done with an altruistic motivation. You can generate such a motivation by thinking "I am going to do this practice in order to help all beings become free from sufferings such as disease, as well as from the causes of sufferings: delusions and karma."

Visualization Visualize the Medicine Buddha a few inches above the top of your head. He is sitting on a moon disk, which rests in the center of an opened lotus, with his legs crossed in the vajra, or full-lotus, position, and faces the same way as you. His body is made of bright royal-blue light, the color of lapis lazuli. Every aspect of the visualization is made of light and radiates light. His right hand rests on his right knee in the gesture of granting sublime realizations and holds the stem of an *arura* (myrobalan) plant between his thumb and first finger. His left hand, in his lap, is in the gesture of concentration and holds a lapis lazuli bowl filled with nectar. He wears the three saffron robes of a monk, and has all the signs and marks of a fully-enlightened Buddha. His face is peaceful and smiling, looking at all living beings in the universe with compassion and loving-kindness.

Spend some time contemplating the visualization of the Medicine Buddha. Understand that he is the embodiment of all enlightened beings and their sublime qualities. Feel the peace and compassion emanating from him.

If you wish, you can recite the following prayers to generate devotion to the Medicine Buddha and the wish to become a Buddha yourself to benefit all beings:

Refuge and bodhichitta

I go for refuge until I am enlightened
To the Buddha, the Dharma, and the Supreme
Assembly.
By my practice of giving and other perfections,
May I become a Buddha to benefit all sentient beings.
(3 times)

The four immeasurable thoughts

May all sentient beings have happiness and the causes
of happiness;
May all sentient beings be free from suffering and the
causes of suffering;
May all sentient beings be inseparable from the
happiness that is free from suffering;
May all sentient beings abide in equanimity, free from
attachment and anger that hold some close and others
distant.

Prayer to the Medicine Buddha

To the bhagavan, tathagata, arhat, fully enlightened
Buddha Medicine Guru, King of Lapis Light, I prostrate,
go for refuge, and make offerings. May your vow to benefit sentient beings now ripen for myself and others.
(7 times)

Then visualize infinite rays of radiant white light flowing down from the heart and body of the Medicine Buddha. This light fills your body and purifies all disease, afflictions due to spirits or black magic, as well as the cause of these problems: your negative karma, delusions, and mental obscurations. All these negativities leave your body in the form of thick black liquid, like engine oil. Your body becomes as clean and clear as crystal. You can also imagine that all other beings are being purified in the same way.

Ricitation of Mantra Do this visualization while reciting the mantra of the Medicine Buddha:

> *tadyatha om bhaishajye bhaishajye maha bhaishajye raja samudgate svaha* (Which Tibetans pronounce: *tayata om bekanzey bekanzey maha bekanzey radza samungatey soha*). Recite seven times, twenty-one times, or more.

Then recite the mantra again, as many times as you wish, and visualize that the light flowing from the Medicine Buddha fills your body again, bringing all the realizations of the path to enlightenment, and all the qualities of the buddhas and bodhisattvas. You can imagine that the same happens to all other beings. Feel that you and all other beings have actually received all these excellent qualities: that you have received the blessings and inspiration of the Medicine Buddha.

Absorption Finally, visualize that the Medicine Buddha melts into light, which absorbs into your heart. Your mind becomes one with the enlightened mind of all buddhas. Let your mind rest for a while in a state that is completely clear, peaceful, and free from its usual busy thoughts and conceptions. Feel that *this* is your true nature....

Dedication To conclude, dedicate the merit, or positive energy, of the meditation that it may bring true physical and mental health and happiness to all sentient beings, and may be the cause for their eventual attainment of enlightenment. If you wish, you can also recite the following dedication prayers:

Through these merits
May I quickly attain the state of Medicine Buddha,
And lead all living beings, without exception,
Into that enlightened state.

May the supreme jewel bodhichitta
That has not arisen, arise and grow;
And may that which has arisen not diminish
But increase more and more.

Explanation of the mantra

Tadyatha Thus

Om Signifies the enlightened state; the positive qualities of the
   buddhas' bodies, speech and minds.

Bhaishajye Medicine; healing; elimination of pain. Here it signifies healing the pain of our physical and mental sufferings.

Bhaishajye Healing. Here it signifies healing the pain of the
causes   of suffering: delusions and karma.

Maha bhaishajye Great healing. This signifies healing even the
subtle   imprints of disturbing thoughts and emotions.

Raja King

Samudgate Supreme

Svaha May my mind receive, absorb, and keep the blessings of
the mantra, and may they take root in my mind.

6

Meditation on the Eight Verses of Thought Transformation

A good mind, a good heart, and warm feelings are most import-
ant. If you do not have such a good heart, you yourself cannot
function, you cannot be happy, and consequently your family,
children, and neighbors will not be happy either. Thus from
nation to nation and continent to continent, everyone's mind
will become disturbed and people will not be happy.

But if you do have a good attitude, a good mind, a good heart,
the opposite is true. So, in human society, love, compassion, and
kindness are the most important things; they are truly precious.

It is worthwhile making an effort to develop a good, good heart.

—His Holiness the Fourteenth Dalai Lama

Having a good heart means having love—wanting others to be happy—and compassion—wanting them to be free of suffering. To think in this way is the method for achieving our own happiness and the happiness of others. We might know this, but why is it so difficult?

The chief obstacle is our habit of thinking of ourselves first—our self-cherishing attitude. Most of the time we are preoccupied with keeping ourselves happy and comfortable, trying to fulfill our desires, and worrying about our problems, only occasionally finding the energy and the space to really open our hearts to the needs of another.

It is self-cherishing that motivates us to take the biggest piece of cake or the most comfortable chair in the room; to push to the head of the queue or drive as if ours were the only car on the road; to do what we feel like doing without considering how it might affect others. Self-cherishing operates more subtly, too; it lies behind our irritation, pride, jealousy, anxiety, and depression. In fact, just about every time we are unhappy or uneasy it is because we are overly concerned with *me*. We feel that unless we take care of ourselves we will not be happy. In fact, the very opposite is true. Ego's appetite is insatiable—trying to fulfill its wishes is a never-ending job. No matter how much we have, ego continuously grows restless and looks for more. We never reach a point where we feel ultimately satisfied, when we can say, "Now I've had enough." If, on the other hand, we can turn our mind around to think of others and put their needs and desires first, we will find peace. There is a serenity that comes from truly cherishing others. By acting always according to what is least disturbing for others, ego is gradually subdued and our life and relationships take on a new dimension.

But the attitude of cherishing others is not based on disliking oneself or suppressing one's feelings. It is developed by gradually coming to recognize that everyone needs love and wants happiness, just as we do; that every being in the universe is part of one big family, that we all depend on each other, and there is no such thing as an outsider; that self-cherishing brings problems and cherishing others brings peace of mind.

It is not easy to develop universal love and compassion, but as soon as we start trying to do so we will see the changes in our life. We need to persevere, and to be kind to ourselves. At times it may seem that we are not getting any better, but this is only because, with deeper conscientiousness, we are now more aware of our mind, of what has been there all the time. We must remember that it takes time and effort to overcome habits built up over a lifetime—over many lifetimes, in fact!

The Tibetan Buddhist tradition contains many practices for improving our attitudes toward others. This meditation belongs to the thought transformation teachings and practices, which (as discussed in the meditation on tonglen on page 116) are concerned with transforming the attitude of self-cherishing into one of cherishing others. The final aim is the development of bodhichitta, the mind aspiring to reach enlightenment for the sake of all beings.

This practice, composed by Lama Zopa Rinpoche, combines a meditation on Avalokiteshvara, the buddha of compassion, with an eight-verse prayer containing the essence of thought transformation, written by an eleventh century meditation master, Langri Tangpa.

The practice

Motivation Seated comfortably with a quiet, relaxed mind, generate a strong and positive motivation for doing this meditation. Reflect upon the points of the graduated path to enlightenment (page 183) or upon the following:

It is not enough merely to ensure that I avoid suffering in this and future lifetimes.

I must become completely free from cyclic existence, the endless round of death and rebirth.

But this too is inadequate. How can I attain the bliss of liberation, leaving behind all other living beings? Every sentient being has been my mother, not just once but many times in my previous lives, and each has cared for me just like my present mother. (Think of the kindness of your present mother, all that she has done for you from the time you were born. Think that all beings have been as kind as this.)

I have depended upon them for all the happiness I have ever experienced. All the food I eat, the clothes I wear, the books I read, the shelter I have; all the music, movies and other pleasures I enjoy come to me through the kindness of others.

At the moment, these kind sentient beings are experiencing suffering, and, out of ignorance, are creating the causes for future misery.

Recall the lives of people you know—relatives, friends, and neighbors. What problems, physical and mental, are they experiencing? Just as you do not want problems and pain, neither do they. Just as you want happiness and peace of mind, so do they. But do they have any solutions? Do they have any methods to achieve the happiness they want and avoid the suffering they do not want?

Generate the determination to take responsibility for freeing *all* sentient beings from their suffering and leading them to the bliss of enlightenment. But to accomplish this you yourself must be enlightened.

Enlightenment is not without causes and conditions. The principal cause is the loving and compassionate mind of bodhichitta.

Therefore I shall practice the profound teaching on training the mind in bodhichitta.

Visualization Visualize at the level of your forehead, a body's length away, Avalokiteshvara, the buddha of compassion (see picture, page 156). If you have a spiritual teacher, think that Avalokiteshvara is the manifestation of and inseparable from him or her.

His body is of pure white light and radiates rainbow light of five colors: white, red, blue, green, and yellow. He has a gentle smile and looks at you and all other beings with eyes of the greatest compassion.

He has four arms. The hands of the first two are together at his heart and hold a precious jewel that is capable of fulfilling the wishes of every living being. His other right hand holds a crystal rosary and his other left a white lotus. He is seated in the vajra posture on a lotus and a moon disk and is surrounded by the full moon as his aura.

He wears exquisite silk clothes and precious jeweled ornaments. An antelope skin covers his left shoulder and breast. The entire visualization is of radiant light.

(See page 175 for an explanation of the following prayers.)

The seven limbs

> Reverently, I prostrate to Guru Avalokiteshvara with
>   my body, speech and mind;
> I present clouds of every type of offering, actual and
>   imagined;
> I declare all my negative actions accumulated since
>   beginningless time
> And rejoice in the merit of all holy and ordinary beings.
> Please, remain until the end of cyclic existence
> And turn the wheel of Dharma for living beings.
> Because of the merits of myself and others, may the two
>   bodhichittas ripen,
> And may I receive the great enlightenment for the sake
>   of all sentient beings.

Mandala offering

> This ground, anointed with perfume, strewn with
>   flowers,
> Adorned with Mount Meru, four continents, the sun and
>   the moon:
> I imagine this as a buddhafield and offer it.
> May all living beings enjoy this pure land.

Prayer of request

> May the guru's life be long.
> May all beings throughout infinite space receive
>   happiness and comfort.
> May I and all others, without exception,
>   accumulate merit,
> Purify all obscurations, and quickly attain
>   enlightenment.
> Precious guru, please grant me blessings that my mind
>   will become Dharma,
> That Dharma will become the path,
> That hindrances in the path may not occur,

That I may cease all wrong conceptions
And receive immediately the two precious bodhichittas.

Idam guru ratna mandalakam niryatayami
I send forth this jewelled mandala to you precious gurus.

Avalokiteshvara is extremely pleased with your request and upon
his lotus and moon seat descends to the crown of your head.

The Eight Verses of Thought Transformation

Recite the verses, concentrating on their meaning. Spend as long
as you like on each one.

With each verse, visualize a stream of blissful white nectar
pouring out from the syllable *hri* at Avalokiteshvara's heart,
flowing into your body through the crown of your head. It fills
you completely, purifying all your negativities and obscurations
and bringing all realizations—in particular the obscurations and
realizations mentioned in the verse you are meditating upon.

1. With the thought of attaining enlightenment
   For the welfare of all beings,
   Who are more precious than wish-fulfilling jewels,
   I will constantly practice holding them dear.

Living beings are precious because without them we would have
no opportunity to develop generosity, love, patience, and other
altruistic qualities or to overcome our selfishness.

The nectar from Avalokiteshvara purifies the self-cherishing
thought that prevents me from holding others more dear and
bestows the realization of cherishing others more than myself.

2. Whenever I am with others
   I will practice seeing myself as the lowest of all,
   And from the very depths of my heart
   I will hold others dear and supreme.

This is a powerful way to counteract our habitual tendency toward finding fault in others and criticizing them. Instead, we should continually recognize their good qualities and potential, and recall our own faults and shortcomings.

The nectar purifies pride and self-cherishing and brings the realization of bodhichitta, which regards others as dear and supreme.

3. In all actions I will examine my mind and
The moment a delusion arises,
Endangering myself and others,
I will confront and avert it without delay.

This verse stresses the importance of mindfulness. Throughout the day, in everything we do—working, talking, watching television, meditating—we should be aware of what is happening in our mind. Whenever a negative thought like anger, jealousy, or pride arises, we should take note of it and deal with it as soon as possible. If we do not practice like this, delusions remain in the mind, grow stronger, and pollute our every feeling and perception.

The nectar purifies the obscurations that prevent me from confronting and dealing with unsubdued thoughts and brings the realization of bodhichitta and the wisdom of emptiness, which extinguish such thoughts.

4. Whenever I meet a person of bad nature
Who is overwhelmed by negative energy and intense suffering,
I will hold such a rare one dear,
As if I had found a precious treasure.

It is not very difficult to have positive feelings toward people who are kind and good-natured, but our love is really put to the test when we meet people with much negative energy. Because they give us the chance to see how strong our patience and compassion are—and thus bring us down to earth as far as our spiritual development is concerned—we should regard them as rare and precious.

The nectar purifies the self-cherishing thought that prevents me from regarding harmful beings as precious and dear, and brings the realization of bodhichitta, which holds even harmful beings dear.

5. When others, out of jealousy,
    Mistreat me with abuse, slander, and scorn,
    I will practice accepting defeat
    And offering the victory to them.

When someone criticizes us, to our face or behind our back, we should not angrily try to defend ourselves or hurl abuse in return. Instead we should remember that any bad experience is the natural outcome of our own past actions—we can probably think of many instances when we criticized others.

We can try to talk with the person who is complaining—not with anger but compassion—to get them to calm down and think more positively, but if they refuse to be reasonable we should just let go and accept the situation. Anyway, it is good to listen with an open mind to criticism—it is often correct and it can always teach us something about ourselves.

The nectar purifies the self-cherishing thought that prevents me from accepting defeat and giving the victory to others, and brings the realizations that enable me to do this.

6. When someone I have benefited
    And in whom I have placed great trust
    Hurts me very badly,
    I will practice seeing that person as my supreme teacher.

Every good or bad experience that occurs in our life is the result of our past actions, so there is really no such thing as undeserved harm. This idea may be difficult to accept, especially when the harm comes from someone we have helped and from whom we expect at least gratitude. But it is a question of becoming familiar with the law of cause and effect—we must necessarily have created the cause to be harmed. Also, if we have good understanding of the importance of developing patience, we will be able to see that someone who harms us is giving us a valuable teaching on the spiritual path.

The nectar purifies the self-cherishing thought that prevents me from regarding harmful beings as my spiritual teachers, and brings the attainment of the bodhisattva's perfection of patience, which enables me to do this.

7. In short, I will offer directly and indirectly
   Every benefit and happiness to all beings, my mothers.
   I will practice in secret taking upon myself
   All their harmful actions and suffering.

The essence of thought transformation is exchanging self for others—replacing the attitude of cherishing oneself with that of cherishing others. Normally we work on making ourselves happy and avoiding problems, even if it means hurting others, but here we reverse our priorities; we aspire to give happiness to others and to take on their problems, indifferent to our own welfare. This meditation is an internal one, involving a change in our state of mind; it is therefore "secret," not something that everyone can see us practicing.

The nectar purifies the self-cherishing thought that prevents me from taking upon myself all beings' harmful actions and sufferings, and brings the realization of bodhichitta, which offers happiness to them and takes on their suffering.

8. Through perceiving all phenomena as illusory I will keep
   these practices
   Undefiled by the stains of the eight worldly concerns,
   And, free from clinging, I will release all beings
   From the bondage of the disturbing unsubdued mind
   and karma.

When our motivation for doing something involves any of the eight worldly concerns—attachment to pleasure, praise, gain, and fame, and aversion to pain, blame, loss, and notoriety—the action is non-dharma, non-spiritual. By realizing the illusory, dream-like nature of all things and all situations, we naturally learn to let go and cling less tightly to such concerns.

The final aim of this practice is to free ourselves from ignorance, self-cherishing, and all negative energy in order to help others become free, too.

The nectar purifies the self-cherishing thought and self-grasping ignorance that prevent me from seeing all things as illusory, and brings the realization of emptiness, which frees me from the bondage of the unsubdued mind and karma.

Completion Make the following request from the depths of your heart.

> To you, greatly compassionate one, I request:
> Please extend your holy hand and lead me and
>   all beings
> To the blissful pure realm after this life.
> Please be our spiritual friend in all lives
> And lead us quickly to enlightenment.

Avalokiteshvara accepts your request. A stream of nectar flows from his heart into you, completely filling your body and mind. All obscurations, negative imprints, and diseases are purified instantly. Your body becomes crystal-clear. Then Avalokiteshvara melts into light and absorbs into you.

Imagine you are now one with Avalokiteshvara; your body, speech, and mind indistinguishably one with his holy body, speech, and mind. You are surrounded in all directions by all sentient beings.

Avalokiteshvara's mantra Now, while reciting the mantra *om mani padme hum*, visualize countless rays of light radiating from your heart, each with a tiny Avalokiteshvara at its tip. These compassionate buddhas settle above the heads of all sentient beings and with streams of nectar purify their negativities and obscurations. Finally, they absorb into the sentient beings, who all become one with Avalokiteshvara.

Dedication

> May all the suffering and causes of suffering
> Of all sentient beings ripen on me now,
> And may all sentient beings receive all my happiness
>   and virtue.

> May the supreme jewel bodhichitta
> That has not arisen, arise and grow;
> And may that which has arisen not diminish
> But increase more and more.

> May I never be discouraged, even for a moment,
> From practicing the deeds of the bodhisattvas for the
>   sake of others,
> By completely renouncing anything done for my
>   own sake
> And by engaging in the holy actions of the kind founder,
>   Shakyamuni Buddha.

> Through these merits
> May I quickly attain the state of the Great
>   Compassionate One,
> And, without exception, lead all mother sentient beings,
> Who are most high and noble, to that enlightened state.

7

Prayer to Tara

Why is it that some people succeed in nearly every-thing they set out to do while others fail constantly? We say that those who succeed are "lucky," but Buddhism explains that in the past they have created the causes to experience their success—otherwise they would not be experiencing it now (see the meditation on karma on page 80).

If we want to meet with fortunate, satisfying experiences we must create the necessary causes. This is true for any activity—whether it be a business venture, sport, or spiritual practice. We tend to find that the more difficult the goal, the greater the obstacles. An effective method for overcoming these problems and achieving success is making prayers and requests to Tara, the Liberator.

Tara is a manifestation of the wisdom, compassion, love and, in particular, the skillful activity of all enlightened beings. Each detail of her image represents a different aspect of the path: for example, her green color symbolizes her ability to act. Her right hand is in the gesture of granting sublime realizations and her left in the gesture of refuge. Her female form demonstrates that enlightenment is attainable by all—women and men alike.

The practice given here involves repetition of a five-line prayer, which is the essence of the prayer known as the Twenty-one Verses in Praise of Tara, and contains her mantra, *om tare tuttare ture svaha* (pronounced *om ta-ray too-ta-ray too-ray so-ha*); see explanation on page 216.

There is a story about how this five-line prayer originated. In the tenth century, the translator for Atisha, the great Indian teacher who lived in Tibet, became ill. Dromtonpa, Atisha's disciple, predicted that if the translator recited the Twenty-one Verses

Tara the Liberator

in Praise of Tara ten thousand times, he would recover from his illness. The man was too sick to recite this long prayer, so Atisha, who had direct communication with Tara, requested her advice. She gave him the five-line prayer, a single repetition of which is equivalent to recitation of the twenty-one verses. The translator completed the ten thousand repetitions and soon after recovered fully from his illness.

This practice has been compiled by Lama Zopa Rinpoche as a way for us to open our hearts to Tara's incredibly kind, inspiring energy.

The practice

Visualize Tara in the space before you, emerald green in color, seated on a lotus and moon. She is a manifestation of all the bud-dhas' omniscience, love, and compassion, and is of the nature of light, not solid or concrete. Her left leg is drawn up, signifying her complete control over desire, and her right leg is extended, indi-cating that she is ready to rise to the aid of all beings. Her left hand is at her heart in the refuge gesture: palm facing outward, thumb and ring finger joined, and the remaining three fingers raised. Her right hand is on her right knee in the gesture of granting sublime realizations: palm facing outward, with the fingers loosely point-ing down. In each hand she holds the stem of a blue utpala flower, symbol of the unblocking of the central channel. She is beautifully adorned with silk garments and jewel ornaments, and her smiling face radiates love and compassion.

All sentient beings, in human form, surround you: the people you are close to are behind you, those you do not like are in front of you, and all the rest are on either side of you. You are com-pletely surrounded by all sentient beings, as far as the eye can see. Everyone joins you in reciting the following prayers.

Refuge and bodhichitta motivation

I go for refuge until I am enlightened
To the Buddha, the Dharma and the Supreme Assembly.

By my practice of giving and other perfections,
May I become a Buddha to benefit all sentient beings.
(3 times)

The four immeasurable thoughts

May all sentient beings have happiness and the causes
of happiness;
May all sentient beings be free from suffering and the
causes of suffering;
May all sentient beings be inseparable from the happiness that is free from suffering;
May all sentient beings abide in equanimity, free from
attachment and anger that hold some close and others
distant.

The seven limbs

Reverently, I prostrate with my body, speech and mind;
I present clouds of every type of offering, actual and
imagined;
I declare all my negative actions accumulated since
beginningless time
And rejoice in the merit of all holy and ordinary beings.
Please, remain until the end of cyclic existence
And turn the wheel of Dharma for living beings.
I dedicate my own merits and those of all others to the
great enlightenment.

Mandala offering

This ground, anointed with perfume, strewn with flowers,
Adorned with Mount Meru, four continents, the sun and
the moon:
I imagine this as a buddhafield and offer it.
May all living beings enjoy this pure land!

Idam guru ratna mandalakam niryatayami
I send forth this jeweled mandala to you precious gurus.

Prayer to Tara

Now recall any special request you want to make—success in your spiritual or worldly activities, the health and long life of your relatives, friends, or yourself, or anything at all that you want. With these needs in mind, recite the short prayer to Tara as many times as you can, while either remaining seated or making prostrations.

> *Om* I prostrate to the goddess foe destroyer,
>   liberating lady Tara,
> Homage to *tare*, savioress, heroine,
> With *tuttare* dispelling all fears,
> Granting all benefits with *ture*,
> To her with sound *svaha*, I bow.

As you recite the prayer visualize rays of light with nectar running down them (like raindrops running down a wire) emanating from the point where Tara's left thumb and ring finger touch. The rays and nectar flow continuously, reaching you and all the beings surrounding you, purifying your hindrances to Dharma practice and the obscurations to liberation and enlightenment.

Remember the problems of all the people you are praying for. Think also of the sufferings and troubles being experienced by the sentient beings surrounding you: people fighting wars, feeling ill or lonely; those full of anger, pride, or jealousy. As the rays and nectar enter their bodies and minds, their suffering and the causes of their suffering are completely extinguished. All sentient beings become totally liberated.

Think with deep conviction that Tara has accepted your requests and answered your prayers. During the first half of your recitation you can visualize the purification described above, and during the second half you can visualize that you and all beings become one with Tara: with each prayer an identical Tara emanates from the Tara visualized in front of you and dissolves into you and everyone else. You all become completely one with Tara's holy body, speech, and mind.

Dedication

> Due to the merits of these virtuous actions
> May I quickly attain the state of Tara
> And lead all living beings, without exception,
> Into that enlightened state.

> May the supreme jewel bodhichitta
> That has not arisen, arise and grow;
> And may that which has arisen not diminish,
> But increase more and more.

Explanation of the mantra

Om contains three sounds: *ah, oh,* and *mm,* and signifies the immeasurable qualities of the enlightened beings' holy bodies, speech, and minds. According to the tantric teachings of Buddha, the paths included in the mantra *om tare tuttare ture svaha* lead to the omniscient state of mind. By actualizing these paths in our mind we purify our body, speech, and mind and transform them into Tara's holy body, speech, and mind.

Here, *om* is the goal and *tare tuttare ture* is the path.

Tare: "She who liberates." Usually, "Tara" means to liberate from unfortunate rebirths, the sufferings of cyclic existence, and the subtle trap of nirvana.

Although one might become free from cyclic existence and attain nirvana, it takes a long time to rouse oneself from this blissful state of peace and begin to work for sentient beings. Compared with the motivation of attaining enlightenment in order to work for others, the goal of attaining nirvana for oneself alone is limited. Thus Tara frees us not only from cyclic existence but also from the blissful state of peace and leads us to enlightenment.

This is the usual meaning of the first *tare* in the mantra. It represents everything from which we should be liberated, the path that liberates, and the goal to which Tara leads us: the omniscient state of enlightenment.

Here, however, the meaning of *tare* is explained as being liberation from cyclic existence, the first of the four truths—suffering.

Tuttare: "Who eliminates all fears." Tara is said to free us from eight "fears," or the sufferings of eight kinds of delusion, each of which is compared to an external cause of fear: the suffering of attachment, which is like a great flood; the suffering of anger, which is like fire; the suffering of ignorance, which is like an elephant; the suffering of jealousy, which is like a snake; the suffering of pride, which is like a lion; the suffering of miserliness, which is like imprisoning chains; the suffering of wrong views, which is like a thief; and the suffering of doubt, which is like a ghost. If we take refuge in Tara, recite her mantra, and practice her method, she will release us from not only the internal sufferings of the delusions but also from external dangers such as floods, fires, and thieves.

Thus, with *tuttare* Tara liberates us from the true causes of suffering (the second of the four noble truths)—karma, and the delusions that give rise to karma. By reciting it, our fears can be dispelled, which indicates that Tara leads us to the true path, the absolute Dharma—the actual remedy for the causes of suffering.

Ture: "Who grants all success." Here, success refers to the goals of practitioners having the three levels of motivation: a fortunate birth, the goal of the initial level of motivation; nirvana, the goal of the intermediate level of motivation; and enlightenment, the goal of the highest level of motivation. "All success" also refers to success in all pursuits of this life—in relationships, in business, in finding perfect conditions for our Dharma practice, and in accomplishing our Dharma goals.

Svaha: Each word of the mantra from *om* to *svaha* performs a particular function, as explained above; each brings great benefit. Thus "to *svaha* and the other syllables we offer the greatest homage."

Svaha itself means "May the blessings of Tara that are contained in the mantra *om tare tuttare ture* take root in our hearts." If we want to grow apples in our garden, we should plant the root of an apple tree. Similarly, if we want to attain enlightenment we should plant in our heart the root of the complete path, which is contained in the mantra *om tare tuttare ture svaha*. By praying to Tara and reciting her mantra we receive her blessings; through Tara's blessings entering our heart we are able to generate the entire path to enlightenment. By generating the path—method and wisdom—in our minds, our impure body, speech, and mind are purified and transformed into Tara's holy body, speech, and mind.

8

Vajrasattva Purification

Why, when we sit down to meditate, does our mind wander helplessly here and there? Why is it so difficult to control the mind and attain realizations? Perhaps we imagine that things were easier before we started to meditate!

Transforming the mind is not easy, so it is not surprising that we experience obstacles and problems. It is not that we lack wisdom or the ability to meditate properly, to penetrate deep into the mind; rather, we are distracted because of the negative energy of our delusions, our distorted conceptions and emotions, which have been accumulating since beginningless time.

When we sit down to meditate, this energy manifests physically as discomfort or restlessness and mentally as sleepiness, agitation, tension, or doubt. Our weak wisdom-flame exists but is no match for this dark storm of negative energy.

It is possible to still the storm, to purify the negative energy that prevents us from actualizing the path to enlightenment. An especially powerful Vajrayana method is the practice associated with the buddha Vajrasattva (Tibetan: Dorje Sempa). It is said to be as effective in burning away delusions and negative energy as is a great fire in burning away thousands of acres of forest.

One of the characteristics of karma (see page 80), is that it increases with time, in the same way that one fruit seed results in many fruits. It is obvious, then, that to prevent the results of negative actions increasing it is necessary to purify our minds of imprints left by negative actions of body, speech, and mind.

Vajrasattva, the Buddha of Purification

Recitation of the Vajrasattva mantra at least twenty-one times at the end of every day is said to prevent the power of that day's negative karma from increasing. Recitation of the mantra one hundred-thousand times, in the right conditions and with the right state of mind, has the power to purify all negative imprints completely.

Complete purification of our negative karma—which ensures that we will never need to experience the results of our negative actions—depends on strong, pure confession. The four steps in this largely internal practice are known as the four opponent powers (see also page 90).

The two meditations here—by Lama Zopa Rinpoche—combine visualization of Vajrasattva with the four powers; one is done while sitting and the other while prostrating.

The practice while sitting

1. The power of reliance

Visualize about four inches above the crown of your head, an open white lotus bearing a moon disk, upon which is seated Vajrasattva. He is white, translucent and adorned with beautiful ornaments and clothes of celestial silk. Every aspect of this visualization is in the nature of light. He has two hands, crossed at his heart: the right holds a vajra, symbolic of great bliss; the left holds a bell, symbolic of the wisdom of emptiness. The vajra and bell together signify his attainment of the enlightened state, the inseparable unity of the wisdom and form bodies. At his heart is a moon disk with the seed syllable *hum* at its center and the letters of the hundred-syllable mantra of Vajrasattva standing clockwise around its edge.

Holding this visualization clearly in your mind, recite the following prayer.

Refuge and bodhichitta

I take refuge in the sublime precious three;
I will liberate all sentient beings
And lead them to enlightenment;
Thus perfectly do I generate bodhichitta. (3 times)

2. *The power of regret*

Recollect with deep regret the specific negativities you have created. Then meditate deeply on the meaning of the following:

> The negative karma I have accumulated throughout beginningless time is as extensive as the treasury of a great king. Although every negative action leads to countless eons of suffering, it seems that I am constantly striving to create nothing but negative actions. Even though I am trying to avoid nonvirtue and practice positive acts, day and night without respite negativities and moral downfalls come to me like rainfall. I lack the ability to purify these faults so that no trace of them remains; with these negative imprints still in my mind, I could suddenly die and find myself falling to an unfortunate rebirth. What can I do? Please, Vajrasattva, with your great compassion, guide me from such misery!

3. *The power of remedy*

Visualize light radiating in all directions from the *hum* at Vajrasattva's heart, requesting the buddhas to bestow their blessings. They accept the request and send white rays of light and nectar, the essence of which is the knowledge of their body, speech, and mind. This light and nectar fall like a rain of milk and are absorbed into the *hum* and mantra at Vajrasattva's heart. Filling his holy body completely, they enhance the magnificence of his appearance, and increase the brilliance of the mantra until it shines with the light of one hundred-thousand moons reflecting off snowy mountains.

Then, while reciting Vajrasattva's mantra, visualize that white rays of light and nectar stream down continuously from the *hum* and mantra at Vajrasattva's heart. They penetrate the crown of your head, filling your body and mind with infinite bliss.

It is fine to recite the short mantra, *om vajrasattva hum,* but it is highly recommended to use the hundred-syllable mantra.

*om vajrasattva samaya manu palaya / vajrasattva deno patitha
dido may bhawa / suto kayo may bhawa / supo kayo may bhawa
/ anu rakto may bhawa / sarwa siddhi may par ya tsa / sarwa
karma su tsa may / tsi tam shri yam kuru hum / ha ha ha ha
ho / bhagawan / sarwa tathagata / vajra ma may mu tsa / vajra
bhawa maha samaya sattva / ah hum pay /*

Continue reciting the mantra and visualizing the flow of light and
nectar, while also performing the following four visualizations
in turn.

Purification of body Your delusions and negativities in general,
and particularly those of the body, take the form of black ink, and
sicknesses and afflictions caused by spirits take the form of scorpi-
ons, snakes, frogs, and crabs. Flushed out by the light and nectar,
they all leave your body through the lower openings, like filthy
water flowing from a drain-pipe. You are now completely emptied
of these problems; they no longer exist anywhere.

Purification of speech Your delusions and the imprints of negativities of speech take the form of liquid tar. The light and nectar
fill your body as water fills a dirty glass: the negativities, like the
dirt in the glass, rise to the top and flow out through the upper
openings of your body. You are completely emptied of these problems; they no longer exist anywhere.

Purification of the mind Your delusions and imprints of mental
negativities appear as darkness at your heart. When struck by the
forceful stream of light and nectar, the darkness instantly disappears. You are completely emptied of these problems; they no
longer exist anywhere.

Simultaneous purification Finally, visualize these three purifi-
cations simultaneously; they sweep away the subtle obscurations
that prevent you from seeing correctly all that exists. You are completely emptied of these problems; they no longer exist anywhere.

If you are short of time, or just lazy, and unable to do the preceding
visualizations, there is a simplified, alternative visualization:

All the delusions and negativities that you have collected over beginningless lifetimes appear as darkness at your heart. As you recite the mantra, immeasurable, powerful rays of white light and nectar pour down from Vajrasattva's heart and penetrate the crown of your head. Instantly, the darkness at your heart is dispelled, just as the darkness in a room vanishes the moment a light is switched on.

4. The power of resolve

Make the following promise to Vajrasattva, specifying the period for which you intend to keep it:

"I will not create these negative actions from now until...."

Vajrasattva is extremely pleased and says: "Child of the essence, all your negativities, obscurations, and degenerated vows have now been completely purified."

Then Vajrasattva melts into light and dissolves into you. Your body, speech, and mind become inseparably one with Vajrasattva's holy body, speech, and mind.

At the conclusion of the meditation, recite the following prayers:

> Due to the merits of these virtuous actions
> May I quickly attain the state of Vajrasattva,
> And lead all living beings, without exception,
> Into that enlightened state.
>
> May the supreme jewel bodhichitta
> That has not arisen, arise and grow;
> And may that which has arisen not diminish
> But increase more and more.

The practice while prostrating

1. The power of reliance

Visualize Vajrasattva in front of you, and all sentient beings in human form surrounding you. Take refuge and think:

In order to transform my body, speech, and mind into the holy body, speech, and mind of Vajrasattva for the sole purpose of enlightening all mother sentient beings, with great respect I will now make prostrations.

2. The power of regret

Recollect with deep regret the negativities you have created with body, speech, and mind.

3. The power of remedy

While you prostrate, recite the Vajrasattva mantra. Visualize the mantra as a stream of white letters, made of light, flowing from a white *om* at Vajrasattva's brow and absorbing into your own brow, completely purifying the obscurations of your body.

At the same time, visualize the mantra as a stream of red letters, made of light, flowing from a red *ah* at Vajrasattva's throat and dissolving into your own throat, completely purifying the obscurations of your speech.

Simultaneously, visualize the mantra as a stream of blue letters, made of light, flowing from a blue *hum* at Vajrasattva's heart and dissolving into your own heart, completely purifying the obscurations of your mind.

As you purify yourself in this way, visualize all sentient beings around you also prostrating and purifying their own bodies, speech, and minds.

After each prostration, a replica of Vajrasattva absorbs into you and every other being. Think that your body, speech, and mind and those of all beings have been completely purified and are one with Vajrasattva's holy body, speech, and mind.

4. The power of resolve

At the end of the session, make the promise never to engage in these negativities again, visualize Vajrasattva dissolving into you and all sentient beings, and dedicate the merit of the practice with the two dedication prayers, as explained above (page 216).

Explanation of the mantra

Om Signifies the qualities of the buddhas' bodies, speech, and
     minds. It also stands for what is auspicious and of highest
     value.

Vajrasattva (Tibetan: Dorje Sempa) The courageous one who has
     inseparable transcendent wisdom.

Samaya A pledge that cannot be transgressed.

Manu palaya Lead me along the path you took to enlightenment.

Vajrasattva deno pa To be closer to the vajra holy mind.

Titha Please make me abide.

Dido Firm; stable because of its relations to the absolute nature.

May bhawa Please grant me the ability to realize the nature of
     phenomena.

Suto kayo may bhawa Please have the nature of being exceedingly
     pleased with me.

Supo kayo may bhawa May I be in the nature of the highly
     developed great bliss.

Anu rakto may bhawa Please be in the nature of the love that
     leads me to your state.

Sarwa siddhi may par ya tsa Please grant me all the actual
     attainments.

Sarwa karma su tsa may Please grant me all the virtuous actions.

Tsi tam shri yam kuru Please grant me all your glorious qualities.

Hum Seed syllable signifying the vajra holy mind.

Ha ha ha ha ho Signifies the five transcendent wisdoms.

Bhagawan One who has destroyed every obscuration, attained
     all realizations, and passed beyond all suffering.

Sarwa tathagata All those who have gone into the space of
     emptiness just as it is.

Vajra Inseparable.

Ma may mu tsa Do not abandon me.

Vajra Bhawa The nature of inseparability.

Maha samaya sattva The great courageous one having the pledge,
     the holy mind.

Ah Seed syllable signifying the vajra holy speech.

Hum Signifies the transcendent wisdom of great bliss.

Pay Clarifies our understanding of the transcendent wisdom of
   inseparable bliss and emptiness. It also destroys the dualistic
   mind that is opposite to that wisdom.

In summary, the mantra means: O great courageous one whose
holy mind is in the vajra nature of all buddhas, having destroyed
every obscuration, attained all realizations and passed beyond all
suffering, gone just as it is—do not forsake me but liberate me,
please, according to your pledge.

9

The Eight Mahayana Precepts

Keeping vows, or precepts, of morality is the most effective way to remove hindrances to spiritual realizations. Hindrances are the imprints left on our mindstream by unskillful actions of body, speech, and mind. By consciously avoiding negative actions we naturally cease creating more hindrances and purify those of the past, thus clearing our mind for the attainment of realizations.

There are various levels of vows in Buddhism, such as the vows of full ordination taken for life by monks and nuns, the vows of novice monks and nuns, and vows taken by lay people. The taking of vows in a formal ceremony before one's teachers or the visualized buddhas is considered to have more power and meaning for the mind than simply avoiding certain actions in an informal way. Furthermore, if the vows are taken with the Mahayana motivation of bodhichitta, that is, for the welfare of all living beings, the beneficial results are infinite.

It is important to study the benefits of keeping vows and the disadvantages of breaking them (explained below) so that when you do take vows you have full understanding of what you are doing.

The Eight Mahayana Precepts are a set of vows that anyone can take for a period of twenty-four hours. They can be taken any time, but the days of the new, full, and quarter moons are recommended. The ceremony should be performed early in the morning, before dawn (or "while it is still too dark to see the lines on the palm of your outstretched hand"), and the vows should be maintained until dawn the following day.

The first time you take the precepts you should do so from a person who has received the oral transmission of the practice, regarding that person as Buddha and imagining that you are making your promises to him or her. Thereafter, you can perform the ceremony yourself, reciting the prayers before an image of your teacher or the Buddha, again imagining that you are taking the vows from Buddha himself.

If you break any of the vows during the day, you should purify the transgression as soon as possible with the four opponent powers (see pages 90 or 219). Increased familiarity with keeping precepts will lessen the chances of careless, unconscious transgression.

The benefits of keeping precepts Buddha has said, "Keeping precepts is much more beneficial than making many offerings to all the buddhas over as many eons as there are grains of sand in the Ganges." And, according to one great Indian pandit, "Keeping the eight precepts for just one day brings greater benefit to performing acts of charity for one hundred years."

By keeping precepts we will develop a clear, uncluttered mind and thus find it easier to meditate; avoid unfortunate rebirths and obtain human rebirths with all the necessary conditions for Dharma practice; and meet perfect teachers in future lives, thereby giving ourselves the opportunity to receive further teachings and attain spiritual realizations. Maitreya, the future buddha, said, "Any follower of Shakyamuni Buddha who keeps the eight precepts will be reborn as one of those around me." And we will attain liberation from cyclic existence and finally the goal of enlightenment, actualizing the knowledge and perfections of the Buddha's holy body, speech, and mind.

The disadvantages of breaking precepts Having promised not to do a particular negative action and later doing it results in greater negative karma than doing it under ordinary circumstances. This should be clearly understood before we commit ourselves to any vows. Taking and then breaking precepts amounts to lying to the buddhas; moreover, because they are taken in order to benefit all sentient beings, breaking precepts is like lying to all sentient beings as well. Such negligence leaves deep negative imprints on the mindstream that will lead to future misfortune.

If precepts are broken, we will not receive the benefits mentioned above. In addition, we will remain longer in cyclic existence and experience the sufferings of unfortunate rebirths. If we are close to attaining realizations, breaking precepts will cause us to lose the insight we have already developed. It is essential, therefore, to take the precepts seriously and with proper understanding.

The eight precepts

1. To avoid killing, that is, causing the death of another living being directly or indirectly.
2. To avoid stealing, that is, taking something of value that belongs to another without their permission. This includes borrowing with the clear intention not to return the object.
3. To avoid sexual intercourse and any other type of sexual contact, including self-stimulation.
4. To avoid telling lies, that is, deceiving another by your actions of body, speech, and mind, or having someone lie on your behalf. It includes lying by implication, for example, remaining silent in answer to a question, thus allowing someone to draw a false conclusion.
5. To avoid intoxicants, that is, alcohol, tobacco, recreational drugs, and so forth.
6. To avoid eating more than one meal during the twenty-four-hour period. The meal should be taken before noon and once you have stopped eating for more than thirty minutes the meal is considered finished. Thereafter light fluids such as tea and coffee can be taken, but not undiluted whole milk or fruit juice with pulp. You should also avoid eating certain "black" foods, such as meat, fish, eggs, onions, garlic, and radishes.

7. To avoid sitting on a high, expensive bed or seat with pride. Ornate or jeweled seats and animal-skin covers should also be avoided.
8. To avoid wearing jewelry, perfume, and similar adornments, and to avoid singing, dancing, or playing music with attachment.

For a precept to be broken, four conditions must be met:

1. The motivation for the action must be a negative attitude such as attachment, aversion, and so forth.
2. There must be an object of the action, for example, a being that is killed, an object that is stolen, and so forth.
3. One must carry out the action or tell another to do it.
4. The action must be completed, for example, the being you kill must die before you do, or you must have the thought "this is mine" regarding a stolen object.

The heaviness or lightness of the action is determined by the intensity of these four factors. For example, an action motivated by intense anger is more serious than the same action performed out of ignorance; killing a human being is more serious than killing an insect. In order to understand this subject more fully, one should study karma, the law of cause and effect.

The ceremony

Preliminary prayers, said while standing:

Refuge in the guru

The guru is Buddha; the guru is Dharma;
The guru is Sangha also;
The guru is the creator of all (happiness);
To all gurus I go for refuge. (3 times)

Bodhichitta motivation

To accomplish my own and others' aims,
I generate the mind seeking enlightenment. (3 times)

Purifying the environment

Everywhere may the ground be pure,
Free of the roughness of pebbles and so forth.
May it be in the nature of lapis lazuli
And as smooth as the palm of one's hand.

Offering prayer

May human and divine offerings,
Actually arranged and mentally created,
Clouds of finest Samantabhadra offerings,
Fill the entire space.

Mantra to bless and increase the offerings

*om namo bhagavate vajra sara pramardane / tathagataya / arhate
samyaksam buddhaya / tadyatha / om vajre vajre / maha vajre
/ maha teja vajre / maha vidya vajre / maha bodhichitta vajre
/ maha bodhi mändo pasam kramana vajre / sarva karma / ava
rana visho dhana vajre svaha /* (3 times)

Expressing the power of truth

By the power of truth of the Three Rare Sublime Ones,
the blessings of all the buddhas and bodhisattvas,
the great wealth of the completed two collections,
and the sphere of phenomena being pure and
inconceivable; may these piles of clouds of offerings
arising through transformation by the bodhisattvas
Arya Samantabhadra, Manjushri, and so forth—unimag-
inable and inexhaustible, equaling the sky—arise and,
in the eyes of the buddhas and bodhisattvas of the ten
directions, be received.

Invocation

Protector of all beings without exception,
Divine destroyer of the intractable legions of Mara;
Perfect knower of all things:
Bhagavan and retinue, please come here.

Now do three prostrations while repeating the mantra:

*om namo manjushriye namah sushriye nama uttama shriye
svaha*

(translation, not to be recited: *om* homage to the glorious
lovely one; homage to the very glorious; homage to the
most glorious *svaha*)

Now repeat the following three times with prostrations, then sit
down:

To the guru, founder,
Bhagavan, tathagata, arhat,
Perfectly completed buddha,
Glorious conqueror Shakyamuni Buddha
I prostrate, make offerings, and go for refuge.
Please grant me your blessings.

The seven limbs

Reverently, I prostrate with my body, speech, and mind;
I present clouds of every type of offering, actual and
    imagined;
I declare all my negative actions accumulated since
    beginningless time
And rejoice in the merit of all holy and ordinary beings.
Please, remain until the end of cyclic existence
And turn the wheel of Dharma for living beings.
I dedicate my own merits and those of all others to the
    great enlightenment.

Mandala offering

> This ground, anointed with perfume, strewn with
>   flowers,
> Adorned with Mount Meru, four continents, the sun,
>   and the moon:
> I imagine this as a buddhafield and offer it.
> May all living beings enjoy this pure land!
> The objects of my attachment, aversion, and ignorance—
>   friends, enemies and strangers—
> And my body, wealth, and enjoyments;
> Without any sense of loss, I offer this collection.
> Please accept it with pleasure
> And bless me with freedom from the three poisons.

> *Idam guru ratna mandalakam niryatayami*
> I send forth this jeweled mandala to you precious gurus.

Taking the ordination

Now stand up and make three prostrations. Then, kneel on your right knee with your hands together in prostration and your head bowed. Visualize Guru Avalokiteshvara before you, generate the profound bodhichitta motivation for taking the precepts, and repeat three times:

> All buddhas and bodhisattvas dwelling in the ten direc-
> tions, please pay attention to me. Just as the previous
> tathagathas, foe destroyers, perfectly completed buddhas,
> who, like the divine wise horse and the great elephant,
> did what had to be done, performed actions, laid down
> the burden, subsequently attained their own welfare,
> completely exhausted the fetters to existence, and had
> perfect speech, well-liberated minds, and well-liberated
> wisdom, for the welfare of all sentient beings, in order to
> benefit, in order to liberate, in order to eliminate famine,
> *in order to eliminate war, in order to stop the harm of the four*
> *elements,* * in order to eliminate sickness, in order to fully

complete the thirty-seven practices harmonious with enlightenment, and in order to definitely actualize the unsurpassed result of perfect, complete enlightenment, perfectly performed the restoring and purifying ordination; similarly, also I, who am called [*say your name*], from this time until sunrise tomorrow, for the welfare of all sentient beings, in order to benefit, in order to liberate, in order to eliminate famine, *in order to eliminate war, in order to stop the harm of the four elements,** in order to eliminate sickness, in order to fully complete the thirty-seven practices harmonious with enlightenment, and in order to definitely actualize the unsurpassed result of perfect, complete enlightenment, shall perfectly undertake the restoring and purifying ordination.

Upon completing the third recitation, think that you have received the vows in your continuum and rejoice. Then regenerate the thought of bodhichitta, the altruistic aspiration to attain enlightenment for the sake of all sentient beings, by thinking:

> Just as the foe destroyers of the past have abandoned all misconduct of body, speech, and mind, such as taking the lives of others, so shall I, for the sake of all beings, abandon for one day these wrong actions and devote myself to the pure practice of the training.

The commitment prayer to keep the precepts

> From now on I shall not kill, steal others' possessions, engage in sexual activity, or speak false words. I shall avoid intoxicants, from which many mistakes arise. I shall not sit on large, high, or expensive beds. I shall not eat food at the wrong times. I shall avoid singing, dancing, and playing music, and I shall not wear perfumes, garlands, or ornaments. Just as the arhats have avoided

---

* The phrases "in order to eliminate war" and "in order to stop the harm of the four elements" were added to the original text by Lama Zopa Rinpoche.

wrong actions such as taking the lives of others, so shall
I avoid wrong actions such as taking the lives of others.
May I quickly attain enlightenment, and may the living
beings who are experiencing the various sufferings be
released from the ocean of cyclic existence.

The mantra of pure morality (to purify broken precepts)

*om ahmogha shila sambhara / bhara bhara / maha shuddha sattva
padma bibhushita budza / dhara dhara / samanta / avalokite hum
phat svaha* (21 times)

Dedication prayers

May I maintain faultless morality of the rules
And immaculate morality.
May the perfection of moral conduct be completed
By keeping morality purely and untainted by pride.

May the supreme jewel bodhichitta
That has not arisen, arise and grow;
And may that which has arisen not diminish
But increase more and more.

In all my lives, never separated from perfect gurus,
May I enjoy the magnificent Dharma.
By completing the qualities of the stages and paths,
May I quickly attain the state of Vajradhara.

Because of the merits of taking the ordination and
    keeping the precepts,
May I and all sentient beings achieve the two
    enlightened holy bodies
Created by the two vast accumulations of merit and
    transcendental wisdom.

Just as the brave Manjushri and Samantabhadra, too,

Realized things as they are,
I, too, dedicate all these merits in the best way,
That I may follow their perfect example.

I dedicate all these roots of virtue
With the dedication praised as the best
By the victorious ones thus gone of the three times,
So I might perform good works.

Make three prostrations to conclude the ceremony.

Then think:

This is my contribution to the peace and happiness of all
sentient beings and, in particular, to the peace and happiness of all the sentient beings of this world. *(From the
instructions of Lama Zopa Rinpoche)*

If you happen to break any of the precepts during the day, feel
regret, and, as soon as possible, do a purification practice with
the four opponent powers (see pages 90 or 219). You can recite
the mantra of pure morality (page 236) twenty-one times for the
power of remedy.

At the end of the day, dedicate the merit of keeping the precepts:

Through these merits, may I quickly attain enlightenment
by realizing renunciation, bodhichitta, and emptiness, for
the sake of all sentient beings.

10

Prostrations to the Thirty-five Buddhas

Pure moral discipline is essential for the realization of the graduated path to enlightenment. Moral discipline, one of the six perfections, or practices of a bodhisattva, entails creating positive actions and refraining from and purifying negative actions and broken vows. The practice of confession and prostrations to the Thirty-five Buddhas (also known as *The Bodhisattva's Confession of Moral Downfalls*) is one of the many methods used for purification.

Negative actions can be purified fully only if the four opponent powers are used (see pages 90 or 219). These four powers are included in the confession prayer: the power of reliance in the explicit expression of refuge in the gurus, buddhas, Dharma, and Sangha; the power of the remedy in the recitation of the names of the Thirty-five Buddhas; the power of regret in the recollection of the negative actions we created in the past, and the power of resolve in the line "...from now on I promise to refrain from these actions." To make the four powers complete, we should begin by generating pure bodhichitta motivation for doing the practice.

This method is especially powerful if practiced first thing in the morning to purify any negativities created during the night, and last thing at night to purify negativities created during the day. The most effective way to use the prayer is to recite it while mentally visualizing the Thirty-five Buddhas and physically making prostrations (see page 177). In this way one's mind, speech, and body all take part in the purification process.

The Thirty-five Buddhas of Confession

The practice

Visualize the Thirty-five Buddhas. Shakyamuni Buddha, the first
buddha, is visualized in the space before you and slightly above
your head. He is seated on a throne decorated with pearls and
supported by a white elephant. Pearl, being white, symbolizes
the complete purification of negativities, and the elephant, being
a powerful animal, symbolizes powerful purification. Buddha sits
in the vajra posture, wearing the robes of a monk; his right hand
is in the earth-touching gesture while his left is in his lap, holding
a bowl filled with nectar.

Thirty-four rays of light emanate out and downward from the
heart of Shakyamuni Buddha. At the tip of each ray is a pearl-dec-
orated throne supported by a white elephant. These thrones are
arranged in five rows beneath Shakyamuni Buddha, and the
thirty-four remaining buddhas are seated on them in the vajra
posture. They are all in the aspect of monks, but the colors and
hand-gestures of the buddhas in each row are different. In the
first row there are six buddhas, dark blue in color (except for the
third Buddha, King, Lord of the Nagas, who has a white face),
and their hand-gestures are the same as Shakyamuni Buddha's.

In the second row there are seven buddhas, white in color, with
their hands in front of their heart, in fists, one above the other, with
index fingers pointing upwards, the upper fist holding the index
finger of the lower.

The seven buddhas in the third row are yellow, with their left
hands in their lap in the meditation pose, and their right hands
in the gesture of granting sublime realizations (like that of Tara,
page 152).

The seven buddhas in the fourth row are red, with both hands
in the meditation pose.

The seven buddhas in the fifth row are green, with their left hands
in the meditation pose and right hands in the gesture of giving
protection (in front of their heart, palm open and facing outwards).

If it is difficult to visualize the different colors and hand-gestures
of all the buddhas, don't worry—just imagine that they are there,
smiling at you compassionately and radiating light.

Saying the names of the Thirty-five Buddhas purifies vast amounts of negative karma and obscurations. If you do not know the names by heart, you can keep the book open on a table next to you, read the name of each buddha and then make a prostration. If you can, repeat the name as many times as possible while prostrating to that buddha. You can do as many prostrations as you wish while reciting the buddhas' names. Then, when you have finished that part of the practice, sit or kneel and read the rest of the prayer.

While prostrating, you can visualize around you all the bodies you have had in your previous lives, as well as all other sentient beings; they are all prostrating along with you. As you recite the prayer, rays of light flow from the buddhas, purifying all negativities of your body, speech, and mind, and those of all the beings around you. Immediately, your negative imprints disappear completely, just as the darkness in a room vanishes the moment a light is switched on. Feel that your body and mind becomes completely empty and pure in nature.

First, make three prostrations, each time reciting the following mantra, which increases the benefit of all your prostrations:

om namo manjushriye namah sushriye nama uttama shriye svaha

Continue to prostrate while reciting the following prayer of refuge three times, and the names of the Thirty-five Buddhas once or three times each:

I, *(say your name)* throughout all times, take refuge in
    the guru;
I take refuge in the Buddha;
I take refuge in the Dharma;
I take refuge in the Sangha. (3 times)

To the Founder, Bhagavan, Tathagata, Arhat, Perfectly
  Completed Buddha, Glorious Conqueror Shakyamuni
  Buddha, I prostrate.
To Tathagata Thoroughly Destroying with Vajra
  Essence, I prostrate.
To Tathagata Radiant Jewel, I prostrate.
To Tathagata King, Lord of the Nagas, I prostrate.
To Tathagata Army of Heroes, I prostrate.
To Tathagata Delighted Hero, I prostrate.
To Tathagata Jewel Fire, I prostrate.
To Tathagata Jewel Moonlight, I prostrate.
To Tathagata Meaningful to See, I prostrate.
To Tathagata Jewel Moon, I prostrate.
To Tathagata Stainless One, I prostrate.
To Tathagata Bestowed with Courage, I prostrate.
To Tathagata Pure One, I prostrate.
To Tathagata Bestowed with Purity, I prostrate.
To Tathagata Water God, I prostrate.
To Tathagata Deity of the Water God, I prostrate.
To Tathagata Glorious Goodness, I prostrate.
To Tathagata Glorious Sandalwood, I prostrate.
To Tathagata Infinite Splendor, I prostrate.
To Tathagata Glorious Light, I prostrate.
To Tathagata Sorrowless Glory, I prostrate.
To Tathagata Son of Non-craving, I prostrate.
To Tathagata Glorious Flower, I prostrate.
To Tathagata Pure Light Rays Clearly Knowing by Play,
  I prostrate.
To Tathagata Lotus Light Rays Clearly Knowing by
  Play, I prostrate.
To Tathagata Glorious Wealth, I prostrate.
To Tathagata Glorious Mindfulness, I prostrate.
To Tathagata Glorious Name Widely Renowned,
  I prostrate.
To Tathagata King Holding the Victory Banner of
  Foremost Power, I prostrate.

To Tathagata Glorious One Totally Subduing, I prostrate.

To Tathagata Utterly Victorious in Battle, I prostrate.

To Tathagata Glorious Transcendence Through
Subduing, I prostrate.

To Tathagata Glorious Manifestations Illuminating All,
I prostrate.

To Tathagata All-Subduing Jewel Lotus, I prostrate.

To Tathagata, arhat, perfectly completed buddha, King
of the Lord of Mountains Firmly Seated on Jewel and
Lotus, I prostrate.

All those [you Thirty-five Buddhas] and others, as many tathaga-
tas, arhats, perfectly completed buddhas as there are existing, sus-
taining, and residing in all the world systems of the ten directions;
all you buddha-bhagavans, please pay attention to me.

In this life and in all the states of rebirth in which I have circled in samsara throughout beginningless lives, whatever negative actions I have created, made others create, or rejoiced in
the creation of; whatever possessions of stupas, possessions of
the Sangha, or possessions of the Sangha of the ten directions
that I have appropriated, made others appropriate, or rejoiced
in the appropriation of; whichever among the five actions of
immediate (retribution) I have done, caused to be done, or
rejoiced in the doing of; whichever paths of the ten nonvirtuous actions I have engaged in, caused others to engage in,
or rejoiced in the engaging in: whatever I have created, being
obscured by these karmas causes me and sentient beings to be
born in the hell realms, in the animal realm, and in the preta
realm; in irreligious countries, as barbarians, or as long-life
gods; with imperfect faculties, holding wrong views, or not
being pleased with Buddha's descent. In the presence of the
buddha-bhagavans, who are transcendental wisdom, who
are eyes, who are witnesses, who are valid, and who see with
omniscient consciousness, I am admitting and confessing
all these negativities; I will not conceal them nor hide them,

and from now on in the future I will abstain and refrain from committing them again.

All buddha-bhagavans, please pay attention to me. In this life and in all other states of rebirth in which I have circled in samsara throughout beginningless lives, whatever roots of virtue I have created by generosity, even as little as giving just one mouthful of food to a being born in the animal realm; whatever roots of virtue I have created by guarding morality; whatever roots of virtue I have created by following pure conduct; whatever roots of virtue I have created by fully ripening sentient beings; whatever roots of virtue I have created by generating bodhichitta; and whatever roots of virtue I have created by my unsurpassed transcendental wisdom: all these assembled and gathered, combined together, I fully dedicate to the unsurpassed, the unexcelled, that higher than the high, that superior to the superior. Thus, I completely dedicate to the highest, perfectly complete enlightenment.

Just as the previous buddha-bhagavans have fully dedicated, just as the future buddha-bhagavans will fully dedicate, and just as the presently abiding buddha-bhagavans are fully dedicating, like that I too dedicate fully.

I confess all negativities individually. I rejoice in all the merits. I urge and implore all buddhas to grant my request: may I receive the highest, most sublime transcendental wisdom.

To the conquerors, the best of humans—those who are living in the present time, those who have lived in the past, and those who will likewise come—to all those who have qualities as vast as an infinite ocean, with hands folded, I approach for refuge.

Dedication

To conclude the practice, dedicate the positive energy you have created to the attainment of enlightenment for the benefit of all living beings. If you wish, you can recite the dedication prayers on page 174.

Dedication

To all beings.
May their confusion cease,
May love and wisdom grow in them.
May they become whole and free.

Glossary

A

altar. Representations, on a table or other surface, of the body, speech, and mind of the **Buddha,** and the offerings that a practitioner makes daily to them.

arhat (Sanskrit). Foe destroyer. One who has attained **liberation.**

arya (Sanskrit). Noble one; a superior being; one who has attained direct insight into **emptiness** and thus cut the root of **cyclic existence.**

attachment. Desire; clinging. The disturbing emotion, or **delusion,** that is the main cause of suffering in day-to-day life, which gives rise to anger, jealousy, pride, depression, and the other delusions.

Atisha. Eleventh-century Indian scholar and meditator who spent the last seventeen years of his life in Tibet; author of many works, including *Lamp for the Path,* which gave rise to the tradition of *lamrim,* the **graduated path to enlightenment**.

B

beginningless lives/mind/time. According to Buddha, there is no creator, and no beginning to the existence of things. Worlds and beings come in and go out of existence according to the natural law of cause and effect. Therefore, time, our mind, and our rebirths are without beginning.

bhagavan (Sanskrit). Epithet of a **buddha,** meaning one who has destroyed all obstacles, is endowed with realizations, and has transcended the world.

bodhichitta (Sanskrit). The aspiration to become a **buddha** in order to benefit all beings, stemming from heartfelt **love** and **compassion.**

bodhisattva (Sanskrit). A being who is striving for **enlightenment** with the motivation of **bodhichitta,** that is, in order to free all other beings from confusion and suffering.

buddha (Sanskrit). An awakened one; a fully enlightened being; one who has achieved perfection and is fully developed in **wisdom** and **compassion** and thus capable of perfectly benefiting every being. The buddha of this age is known as **Shakyamuni.**

buddhafield. Pure land. A state of existence outside **cyclic existence** where all conditions are favorable for becoming enlightened.

buddhahood. See *enlightenment*

C

cause and effect. See *karma*

central channel. According to **tantra,** the principal channel of the psychic nervous system, which runs down from the crown of the head, just in front of the spine.

chakra (Sanskrit). Literally, "wheel." Within the psychic nervous system, any one of the several places along the **central channel** where the energy is constricted.

compassion. Empathy with the suffering of others; the heartfelt wish that they be free of suffering; on the **Mahayana** path, leads to **bodhichitta.**

conventional existence/reality. See *dependent arising*

cyclic existence. (Sanskrit: *samsara*) The cycle of death and rebirth, fraught with suffering and dissatisfaction, the main cause of which is **ignorance.**

D

Dalai Lama, His Holiness the. Temporal and spiritual leader of the Tibetan people, recognized as the human manifestation of Avalokiteshvara, the **buddha** of **compassion.** The current Dalai Lama, fourteenth in the lineage, was born in 1935 and heads the Tibetan government-in-exile in Dharamsala, India.

deity. In **tantra,** a term for a **buddha.**

delusions. Disturbing emotions; negative states of mind; negative thoughts; negative energy; nonvirtuous states of mind. The states of mind such as **attachment,** anger, pride, and depression, arising from the root delusion, **ignorance,** which cause one to suffer and thus to harm others. With **karma,** the main cause of suffering.

dependent arising. Interdependence. The way that all things and beings exist conventionally: they come into being in dependence upon various factors, not from their own side; the proof of their **emptiness.**

Dharma. Spiritual teachings; any technique or knowledge that frees one from suffering and its causes.

E

emptiness. The way that things and beings exist ultimately: that is, they lack (are empty of) inherent existence, existence from their own side, or existence in and of themselves. The **wisdom** developed in meditation on emptiness is the direct opposite of the **ignorance** in the mind that causes us to believe that all things exist inherently.

enlightenment. Buddhahood; perfection; the complete elimination of all **delusions**, including the root **ignorance**, and the development of all positive qualities; the full development of **wisdom** and **compassion.** The innate potential of every living being.

F

faith. Confidence in someone or something that has excellent qualities or abilities.

foe destroyer. See *arhat*

four noble truths. The teaching of **Shakyamuni Buddha** that asserts that (1) there is suffering, (2) there are causes, (3) there is an end to it, and (4) there are means to end it.

four opponent powers. Regret, reliance, remedy, resolve: the four attitudes cultivated in the process of **purification** of negative **karma.**

FPMT. Foundation for the Preservation of the Mahayana Tradition, a worldwide network of Tibetan Buddhist centers and activities, established in 1975 by **Lama Thubten Yeshe** and now under the spiritual guidance of **Lama Thubten Zopa Rinpoche.**

G

graduated path to enlightenment. (Tibetan: *lamrim*). Buddhist teachings outlining the progressive stages of development on the path to enlightenment, originally articulated by the eleventh-century Indian master **Atisha.**

guru (Tibetan: *lama,* meaning "heavy with qualities"). Spiritual teacher.

guru-yoga. The practice of seeing one's **guru** as a **buddha.**

I

ignorance. Not seeing the reality of things. There are various kinds of ignorance, but the principal one is "self-grasping ignorance," the instinctive assumption that self and all things exist inherently, independently, from their own side. This ignorance is the root **delusion,** the main cause of **cyclic existence** and therefore of suffering, and it is counteracted by **wisdom.**

inherent existence. See *ignorance*

inner heat meditation. In **tantra,** a meditation for harnessing **attachment** energy.

K

karma (Sanskrit). Literally, "action." The law of cause and effect: the natural process whereby virtuous actions of body, speech, and mind lead to happiness and nonvirtuous ones to **suffering.**

L

lama (Tibetan). See *guru*

lamrim. See *graduated path to enlightenment*

liberation. (Sanskrit: *nirvana*) Freedom from suffering and its causes (**delusion** and **karma**).

lojong (Tibetan). See *thought transformation.*

lotus position. The cross-legged position recommended for sitting during **meditation** in which each foot, sole upward, is placed on the thigh of the opposite leg.

love. Loving-kindness. The heartfelt wish that others be happy.

M

Mahayana (Sanskrit). Literally, "Great Vehicle." The teachings and practices for those seeking **buddhahood,** motivated by **bodhichitta.**

Maitreya. The next founder-buddha, after Shakyamuni Buddha's **Dharma** has disappeared.

mandala offering. Practice of mentally offering the entire universe. *Inner mandala:* the practice of offering one's **delusions** and the people and things that activate them.

mantra (Sanskrit). Words of power; syllables, usually Sanskrit, recited during certain meditation practices.

meditation (Tibetan: *gom*; literally, "to familiarize"). The process of becoming deeply acquainted with **positive states of mind.**

merit. Positive energy created in the mind by doing virtuous actions with body, speech, and mind.

mindfulness. The capacity of the mind to not forget, from moment to moment, what it is doing, developed and utilized especially in **meditation.**

Mount Meru. According to Buddhist cosmology, the center of the universe.

N

negative state of mind. See *delusions*

nirvana (Sanskrit). See *liberation*

nonvirtue. Negative action, or **karma,** of body, speech, or mind, motivated by **delusions.** Nonvirtue is the cause of suffering.

O

one gone beyond, one thus gone. See *tathagata*

ordination. Formal process of adopting various **vows.**

P

positive state of mind. Positive energy; beneficial state of mind.

preta (Sanskrit). A type of spirit, a **sentient being,** who suffers from extreme hunger and thirst.

pure land. See *buddhafield*

R

refuge. The attitude of relying upon someone or something for guidance and help; in Buddhism one takes refuge in the **Three Jewels**: **Buddha, Dharma,** and **Sangha.**

renunciation. The attitude of complete detachment from the experiences of **cyclic existence,** seeing that there is no true pleasure or satisfaction to be found within it.

S

samsara (Sanskrit). See *cyclic existence*

Sangha. The monastic community following the teachings of **Buddha** (and, more broadly, spiritual friends who support one's practice of **Dharma**); the assembly of **arya** beings on the path to **liberation** and **enlightenment.**

sentient being (Tibetan: *semchen;* literally, "mind-possessor"). Any being in the various realms of **cyclic existence,** such as humans, spirits (**pretas**), and animals, who has not yet attained **liberation** or **enlightenment.**

seven limbs. A sevenfold practice, done extensively or expressed in a seven-line prayer, consisting of prostration, offering, confession, rejoicing, requesting the **buddhas** to stay among sentient beings, requesting the buddha to teach the **Dharma,** and dedication of merit.

Shakyamuni Buddha. Born as a prince in the Shakya family in India approximately 2,500 years ago, "The Sage of the Shakyas" renounced his kingdom and achieved **enlightenment,** teaching the path until he passed away at age eighty.

T

tantra. Vajrayana; Mantrayana. Advanced teachings of **Mahayana** Buddhism that lead the practitioner to the speedy attainment of **enlightenment.**

tathagata. One thus gone; one gone beyond. Epithet of a **buddha,** meaning gone beyond all suffering and its causes (**karma** and **delusion**).

thought transformation (Tibetan: *lojong*). A genre of **Mahayana** teachings or a set of practices that encourages the practitioner to use suffering to combat self-cherishing, or selfishness.

Three Jewels. Three Rare Sublime Ones. The objects of Buddhist **refuge: Buddha, Dharma,** and **Sangha.**

three poisons. The three main **delusions: attachment,** aversion, and **ignorance.**

tonglen (Tibetan). Literally, "giving and taking." Meditation for developing **compassion** and **love** in which one imagines giving others one's happiness (love) and taking upon oneself their suffering (compassion).

Tsongkhapa. Fourteenth-century Tibetan scholar, teacher, and meditator.

U

ultimate nature. See *emptiness*

V

vajra (Tibetan: *dorje*). In tantra, the "diamond-scepter" held by certain **buddhas** that represents **bodhichitta;** often used to mean "indestructible."

vajra posture. See *lotus position*

Vajrayana. The path of **tantra.**

virtue. Positive action, or **karma,** of body, speech, or mind; those actions not motivated by **delusions.**

vows. Sets of commitments relating to the practice of **virtue,** or ethics.

W

wisdom. Specifically, the realization of **emptiness,** developed in meditation, which counteracts **ignorance**.

Y

Yeshe, Lama Thubten (1935–84). Tibetan lama, educated at Sera Monastic University in Lhasa; established the **FPMT** in 1975 in Kathmandu, Nepal.

Z

Zopa Rinpoche, Lama Thubten. Born in Solu Khumbu in 1945, Rinpoche is Spiritual Director of the **FPMT.**

Suggested Further Reading

Introduction to Buddhism

Bodhi, Bhikkhu. *In the Buddha's Words*. Wisdom.
Chodron, Thubten. *Open Heart, Clear Mind*. Snow Lion.
Dalai Lama, The. *The Compassionate Life*. Wisdom.
Hahn, Thich Nhat. *Being Peace*. Parallax.
Kalu Rinpoche. *Luminous Mind*. Wisdom.
Khema, Ayya. *Being Nobody, Going Nowhere*. Wisdom.
Kornfield, Jack. *A Path with Heart*. Bantam.
Rahula, Walpola. *What the Buddha Taught*. Grove Press.
Sogyal Rinpoche. *The Tibetan Book of Living and Dying*.
  Harper.
Suzuki, Shunryu. *Zen Mind, Beginner's Mind*. Weatherhill.
Trungpa Rinpoche. *Cutting Through Spiritual Materialism*.
  Shambhala.
Wallace, B. Alan. *Tibetan Buddhism from the Ground Up*.
  Wisdom.
Yeshe, Lama Thubten and Lama Thubten Zopa Rinpoche.
  Wisdom Energy. Wisdom.

Meditation

Goldstein, Joseph. *The Experience of Insight*. Shambhala.
Gunaratana, Bhante Henepola. *Mindfulness in Plain English*.
  Wisdom.
Hahn, Thich Nhat. *The Miracle of Mindfulness*. Parallax.
Lamrimpa, Gen. *Shamata Meditation*. Snow Lion.
Sharples, Bob. *Meditation and Relaxation in Plain English*.
  Wisdom.

Salzberg, Sharon. *Lovingkindness: The Revolutionary Art of Happiness.* Shambhala.

Wallace, B. Alan. *The Attention Revolution.* Wisdom.

Life of the Buddha

Armstrong, Karen. *Buddha.* Viking.

Hanh, Thich Nhat. *Old Path, White Clouds.* Rider/Parallax.

Kohn, Sherab Chodzin. *The Awakened One: A Life of the Buddha.* Shambhala.

The nature of mind

Rabten, Geshe. *The Mind and Its Functions.* Rabten Choeling.

Graduated path to enlightenment (lamrim)

Dalai Lama, The. *The Path to Enlightenment.* Snow Lion.

Loden, Geshe Thubten. *Path to Enlightenment in Tibetan Buddhism.* Tushita.

Pabongka Rinpoche. *Liberation in the Palm of Your Hand.* Wisdom.

Tsongkhapa. *Principal Teachings of Buddhism.* Mahayana Sutra and Tantra Press.

Wangchen, Geshe. *Awakening the Mind.* Wisdom.

Yangsi Rinpoche. *Practicing the Path.* Wisdom.

Thought transformation (lojong)

Chodron, Pema. *Start Where You Are.* Shambhala.

Dalai Lama, The. *Training the Mind.* Thorsons.

Rabten, Geshe and Geshe Dhargyey. *Advice from a Spiritual Friend.* Wisdom.

Rinchen, Geshe Sonam. *The 37 Practices of Bodhisattvas.* Snow Lion.

Zopa Rinpoche, Lama Thubten. *Transforming Problems into Happiness.* Wisdom

Buddhist/psychotherapy dialogue

Claxton, Guy, et al. *The Psychology of Awakening.* Weiser.
Epstein, Mark. *Thoughts Without a Thinker.* Basic Books.
Goleman, Daniel. *Destructive Emotions.* Bantam.
Moacanin, Radmilla. *The Essence of Jung's Psychology and Tibetan Buddhism.* Wisdom.
Safran, Jeremy (editor). *Psychoanalysis and Buddhism.* Wisdom.

Other books of interest

Dalai Lama, The. *The World of Tibetan Buddhism.* Wisdom.
Mackenzie, Vicki. *Reincarnation.* Wisdom / Bloomsbury.
Mackenzie, Vicki. *Why Buddhism?* Allen & Unwin.
Thondup Tulku. *The Healing Power of Mind.* Arkana.
Yeshe, Lama Thubten. *Introduction to Tantra.* Wisdom.
Zopa Rinpoche, Lama Thubten. *The Door to Satisfaction.* Wisdom.
Zopa Rinpoche, Lama Thubten. *Ultimate Healing.* Wisdom.

Websites

Foundation for the Preservation of the Mahayana Tradition: **www.fpmt.org**

Index

E
eating, 230
effort, too much, 145. *See also*
    joyous effort
ego, 42, 54, 139, 155, 201. *See also*
    ignorance; self-cherishing
Eight Mahayana Precepts,
    228–37
*Eight Verses of Thought
    Transformation,* 205–8
eight worldly concerns, 208–9. *See
    also* attachment
elephant, as symbol, 240
empathy, 130–31, 155. *See also*
    bodhichitta; compassion;
    love; thought transforma-
    tion; tonglen
emptiness. *See also* dependent
    arising; ignorance; inherent
    existence; reality
    as antidote to anger, 132
    as antidote to fear, 139
    and dependent arising, 53, 55,
        57, 82, 110
    explanation of, 53–55
    leading to understanding of, 43
    meditating on, 11, 55–8
    as most powerful remedy, 51,
        70, 98, 126–27
    realization of, 7, 209
    seed of, 175
    sun, as symbol of, 189
endorphins, 136
enemies
    developing compassion for,
        117
    developing equanimity
        toward, 107–10
    developing love for, 114, 130
enlightenment/buddhahood/
    perfection
    Buddha's attainment of, 187

causes of, 175, 177, 193, 203
definition of, 6, 53, 168
as goal, 8, 20–21, 64, 106, 175,
    216, 217. *See also* bodhichitta
making offerings, as cause of,
    178
manifestations of, 144
Milarepa's attainment of, 89
potential for. *See* buddha-na-
    ture
purifying obstacles to, 219
for sake of others, 6, 20–21,
    106, 182, 204. *See also* bodhi-
    chitta
and tantra, 143–44
as woman, 151, 211
equanimity. *See also* bodhi-
    chitta; compassion
immeasurable, 176
method for developing,
    106–10
exchanging self for others, 208.
    See also bodhichitta; com-
    passion; thought transfor-
    mation; tonglen
expectations. *See also* attachment
    causing obstacles to medita-
        tion, 118
    of others, 98, 133
    unrealistic, 3, 8, 17–18, 22, 33,
        51, 145
eyes, open vs closed, 25, 29

F
faith. *See also* devotion; refuge
    understanding, 167
    at the time of death, 78
family
    love for, 112, 114
    at the time of death, 76–77
fear
    dealing with, 137–40

The Foundation for the Preservation of the Mahayana Tradition

The Foundation for the Preservation of the Mahayana Tradition (FPMT) is an international network of Buddhist centers and activities dedicated to the transmission of Mahayana Buddhism as a practiced and living tradition. The FPMT was founded in 1975 by Lama Thubten Yeshe and is now under the spiritual direction of Lama Thubten Zopa Rinpoche. It is composed of Dharma teaching centers, monasteries, retreat centers, publishing houses, healing centers, hospices, and projects for the construction of stupas, statues, and other holy objects.

To receive a listing of these centers worldwide, most of which run meditation classes and retreats, as well as news about their activities, please request a complimentary copy of *Mandala* magazine from:

FPMT International Office
1632 SE 11th Avenue
Portland, OR 97214
USA
Tel: (503) 808-1588
www.fpmt.org

About the Author

Originally from California, Kathleen McDonald (Sangye Khadro) began studying Buddhism with Tibetan lamas in Dharamsala, India, in 1973. She became a nun in Nepal the following year, and received full (bhikshuni) ordination in 1988. At the request of her teachers, she began teaching in 1980, and since then has been teaching Buddhism and meditation in various countries around the world, occasionally taking time off for personal retreats. She served as resident teacher in Buddha House, Australia, for two years and in Amitabha Buddhist Centre in Singapore for eleven years. From 2008–2015 she followed the Masters Program at Istituto Lama Tsong Khapa in Italy. She is also the author of *Awakening the Kind Heart: How to Meditate on Compassion* and coauthor, with Lama Zopa Rinpoche, of *Wholesome Fear: Transforming your Anxiety about Impermanence and Death*, both published by Wisdom Publications.

Also by Kathleen McDonald

Awakening the Kind Heart
How to Meditate on Compassion

"Through clear explanations, straightforward practices, and basic goodheartedness, this book explains how to navigate the path to love, even under very trying circumstances. Truly, there is nothing more needed at this time—our very future may depend upon it."—Susan Piver, author of *The Wisdom of a Broken Heart*

Wholesome Fear
Transforming Your Anxiety about Impermanence and Death
Lama Zopa Rinpoche with Kathleen McDonald

"A wonderful and welcome book for the spiritual well-being of all who read it."—Gelek Rimpoche, author of *Good Life, Good Death*

Also Available from Wisdom Publications

Meditation on Perception
Ten Healing Practices to Cultivate Mindfulness
Bhante Gunaratana

"Yes, he did it again! Bhante G's latest book on the power of perception delivers a profound teaching from the Buddha in clear, precise, everyday language. This book will be of great practical value to all new and experienced meditating yogis."—Larry Rosenberg, author of *Three Steps to Awakening*

Meditation on the Nature of Mind
His Holiness the Dalai Lama, Khonton Peljor Lhundrub, Jose Ignacio Cabezon

"We all have the same human mind—each and every one of us has the same potential. Our surroundings and so forth are important, but the nature of mind itself is more important... To live a happy and joyful life, we must take care of our minds." —His Holiness the Dalai Lama

Mind of Mahamudra
Advice from the Kagyu Masters
Translated and introduced by Peter Alan Roberts

"Quite simply, the best anthology of Tibetan Mahamudra texts yet to appear."—Roger R. Jackson, Carleton College, author of *Tantric Treasures*

The Beautiful Way of Life
A Meditation on Shantideva's Bodhisattva Path
Rene Feusi

"A beautifully written meditative guide to one of the greatest works of the Mahayana Buddhist tradition, and will be treasured by all those inspired by compassion and wisdom."—Jonathan Landaw, author of *Prince Siddhartha*

Introduction to Tantra
The Transformation of Desire
Lama Thubten Yeshe
Edited by Jonathan Landaw, foreword by Philip Glass

"The best introductory work on Tibetan Buddhist tantra available today."—Janet Gyatso, Harvard University

Becoming Vajrasattva
The Tantric Path of Purification
Lama Thubten Yeshe
Edited by Nick Ribush, foreword by Lama Zopa Rinpoche

"[FOUR STARS] Lama Yeshe's instructions are, as always, precious and enormously clarifying and encouraging."—Georg Feuerstein, author of *Tantra: Path of Ecstasy*

About Wisdom Publications

Wisdom Publications is the leading publisher of classic and contemporary Buddhist books and practical works on mindfulness. To learn more about us or to explore our other books, please visit our website at wisdomexperience.org or contact us at the address below.

Wisdom Publications
199 Elm Street
Somerville, MA 02144 USA

We are a 501(c)(3) organization, and donations in support of our mission are tax deductible.

Wisdom Publications is affiliated with the Foundation for the Preservation of the Mahayana Tradition (FPMT).